In these moments
I wonder
at the time spent
in a daze
with the truth
in front of my face.
In the circle's dance
'round the planet's trance
anything could happen
to the human race –
disappear without a trace. . .
and the galaxies
dance on
to the tune played again.
From your door
you step out in trust
that I will be there
for you.
Again.
I never left.
You did
In your desire to experience
what you did not know.

– Dawn Dancing Free

Books by Neale Donald Walsch

Conversations with God, Book 1
Conversations with God, Book 2

Conversations with God

• an uncommon dialogue •

Book 1 Guidebook

Neale Donald Walsch

Cover painting by Louis Jones
Cover design by Marjoram Productions

For information write:

Hampton Roads Publishing Company, Inc.
134 Burgess Lane
Charlottesville, VA 22902

Or call: (804) 296-2772
FAX: (804) 296-5096
e-mail: hrpc@hrpub.com
Website: www.hrpub.com

If you are unable to order this book from your local bookseller, you may order directly from the publisher. Quantity discounts for organizations are available. Call 1-800-766-8009, toll-free.

ISBN 1-57174-048-1

10 9 8 7 6 5 4

Printed in Canada

To
the thousands of readers of
Conversations with God
around the world
who have committed themselves
to exploring at the deepest level
the concepts contained in that document.
Your courage and your willingness
to examine and expand your own life and experience
is an inspiration to me.
You are the real Seekers of Truth,
who are never satisfied
with the surface of things,
but choose more – always more – and
thus create for yourselves
lives which enrich and bless us all.

Acknowledgments

For the entirety of my life, and anything good or decent or creative or wonderful I may have done with it, I thank my dearest friend and closest companion, God.

I have never known such a wonderful friendship – that's exactly what it feels I have going here – and I want never to miss an opportunity to acknowledge it. Some day I hope to explain to everyone in minute detail just how to develop such a friendship, and how to *use it*. For God wants most of all to be used. And that's what we want as well. We want a *friendship with God*. One that's *functional* and *useful*.

Next, I want to thank my publishers (who are very much, come to think of it, like God). I have met few people in my life with the courage and the integrity I have found in Robert S. Friedman, publisher at Hampton Roads Publishing Company, the man who first placed *Conversations with God* before the public by taking a terrific gamble, and Susan Peterson, president of Viking, Penguin and Riverhead books and executive vice president of Penguin-Putnam Inc., who took an equally large gamble by placing the book into hardcover and causing it to be distributed around the world.

I am certain that there are no nicer, more sincere, more literarily sensitive, honest, and powerfully effective people in the publishing industry, and I consider it one of the highest honors of my life to have come to know both of them. Bob and Susan, my thanks can never be enough.

Third, we all know how wonderful it is to have at one's side a person who will not only provide constant and unfailing support, but also inspiration at the lowest moments, wisdom in the most challenging times, practical advice when confusion reigns, and patient, unconditional love even when one cannot love oneself. Of course, finding such an extraordinary person is very rare – unless you have God on your side. In my case, God sent me a great treasure and called her Nancy Fleming-Walsch. She is my lover, my friend, my partner, and my wife. And I am grateful to her beyond measure for all the gifts she has given me.

Our teammates at ReCreation make it possible to achieve the impossible, and only by their doing everything *else* could I have ever been able to put together this Guidebook. My deep gratitude to Dr. William Colson, Una Colson, Richard Crawford, Rita Curtis, Patty Hammett, Tracy Hedgecock, Tricia Matthews, Scott McGuire, Will Richardson, Don St. John, Cherree Weeks, and Rose Wolfenbarger.

I am indebted, too, to Dawn Dancing Free, one of America's sparkling new young poet voices, who speaks of life from a soul which has lived many, and who – like all the really special poets – touches deep places with the movement and the vibration, as well as the content, of her words. Dawn kindly gave me permission to share one offering from her larger work, *Soul Talk*, as an opening to this book.

My final thanks go to Don Stewart of Klamath, California, who found *CWG* so exciting that he came to one of our retreats, then went home and re-read the book line by line in order to help me put together the review questions at the end of each chapter of this Guidebook. While I've added a few, most of the questions were first dreamt up by Don – so if they're a bit tough in places (and also very helpful in increasing your comprehension of the material), you have him to thank for being the meanie at the front of the classroom who will not send you home until you've "learned it all."

To all of these spectacular beings, my humble appreciations are sent.

Introduction

In May of 1995 something extraordinary happened; something which changed the lives of thousands of people, and will change the lives of thousands more for years to come. Indeed, the impact will ultimately affect millions.

In May of 1995 Hampton Roads Publishing Company of Charlottesville, Virginia released a little white book with twelve words on its cover, 76,468 words in its interior, and one simple, elegant thought at the core of its message.

LOVE IS ALL THERE IS

I can say humbly that it is now clear *Conversations with God - Book 1* is a very special document. While there is very little which is new in the book, there is a new way of sharing that which is ancient. For in *Conversations with God*, Deity has spoken to Everyman. . .in Everyman's own language. This has made the wisdom of the ages accessible at last to the average person, perhaps to the largest audience ever.

Within months of the release of this remarkable document (the first volume in a trilogy), informal study groups began forming spontaneously among the people who had read it. They somehow found each other, and began gathering in pockets to pore over the book's marvelous contents. Deeper and deeper into the material they delved, and the more deeply they delved, the more deeply they understood its meaning. Still, there was something more they wished to have. They wished to have an *experience* of its meaning, not merely an understanding. That is, they wished the truths in *Conversations with God* to be rendered *functional* in their daily lives.

This guidebook offers a way to do that. In it, we will take a "guided tour" of the place to which *Conversations with God - Book 1* moves us. And move us it does, to a wonderful place full of peace and of joy, filled with understanding and with love. It is a space of clarity and of deep insight. It is a place where much more is possible than we may have dreamed or imagined.

This is the place within our mind where wisdom dwells, the place within our heart where love resides, the place within our soul where we are home at last.

Many people were transported to this place with a single reading of *CWG*. Yet the real trick is to stay in this place, to never leave it. In an effort to accomplish this, people found themselves reading *CWG* over and over again. And that wasn't a bad idea. Indeed, the book itself suggests it.

But now it's time to go to the next place. Now it's time to not only go *through* the book over and over, but to go deeper *into* it.

That's where this Guidebook takes you.

Allowing This Book to be Experiential

This book is meant to be experiential. There is enough in life that is observational, and there is more than enough that is referential. This books seeks to be something greater than that. It seeks to take you into your own experience.

For that reason, the book contains four ways in which you may interact with it: special inquiries, exercises, assignments, and experiments. In this way the Guidebook invites you to *do stuff, not just read stuff*. The "stuff" it invites you to do may be done alone or as a group with equal value.

Questions with which to jog your mind will appear throughout the book in boxes extending into the margins near the text to which they refer. These **Special Inquiries** offer additional mental explorations you may wish to undertake as you move through the main text. Answering these questions as you go along, either in writing or in your mind, will expand the impact of the text, greatly enhancing your ability to integrate the material. The inside margins of each page have been kept large, allowing you to use them for notes.

The **Exercises** in the book are processes you are invited to undertake while you are reading a chapter or section. That is, you read a bit (in study groups you may wish to take turns reading aloud), do the exercise, read a bit more, do another exercise, and so on. These exercises seek to bring the text alive in an experiential way. Passing over them in order to simply keep reading is not the way to receive the most benefit from this Guidebook.

The **Assignments** and **Experiments** are mini-projects – what might be called "lab work" – which you are invited to complete after finishing a section or chapter. They are for those times between readings (or between study group sessions) when you put the book down. Some of them actually allow you to take the wisdom in the book into the "laboratory of life" – into the "real world" – and try it out, to see what "works" and what "doesn't work" for you. Others call for self-assessments and inner work during the week. All of them seek to bring you back to the book with greater understanding.

This book is an excellent tool for classes or study groups. If you are working through this material as a group, see the section at the end of this introduction on How You May Want to Proceed If You Are in a Study Group. Whether working with a group or individually, it is suggested that you keep a Guidebook journal. In fact, it will be virtually impossible for you to proceed without one. There will be much to write down, much to keep track of, many thoughts that you will wish to save, many processes that require writing, and many times when you will be asked to record your reaction to or comments about a particular assignment, experiment or experience.

If you are working with this book by yourself and not as part of a group, you will find the keeping of a journal even more valuable, for it is here you will place your discussion of the topics, and your answers to the questions, which the Guidebook invites you to address.

Again, the point of the processes through which this book guides you is to *experience* what you know, to *experience* what is true for you, rather than observe, or be referred to, what is true for others.

Religion does that. Religion does not care about your own experience. Religion does not invite you to explore too much of that. In fact, religion steers you away from it. Some religions actually forbid you to question, forbid you to deviate, forbid you to seek your own personal experience. It is the job of religion not to invite you to experience what is true for you, but to *tell you outright* what *should* be true for you.

Politics does that. Politics does not care about your own experience. Politics does not invite you to explore too much of that. In fact, politics steers you away from it. Some political movements actually forbid you to question, forbid you to deviate, forbid you to seek your own personal experience. It is the job of politics not to invite you to experience what is true for you, but to *tell you outright* what *should* be true for you.

Society does that. Society does not care about your own experience. Society does not invite you to explore too much of that. In fact, society steers you away from it. Some societies actually forbid you to question, forbid you to deviate, forbid you to seek your own personal experience. It is the job of society not to invite you to experience what is true for you, but to *tell you outright* what *should* be true for you.

Government does that. Government does not care about your own experience. Government does not invite you to explore too much of that. In fact, government steers you away from it. Some governments actually forbid you to question, forbid you to deviate, forbid you to seek your own personal experience. It is the job of government not to invite you to experience what is true for you, but to *tell you outright* what *should* be true for you.

Education does that. Education does not care about your own experience. Education does not invite you to explore too much of that. In fact, education steers you away from it. Some educators actually forbid you to question, forbid you to deviate, forbid you to seek your own personal experience. It is the job of education not to invite you to experience what is true for you, but to *tell you outright* what *should* be true for you.

All of the above may not be true all of the time, but all of the above is true some of the time. You can tell when these things are happening because that is when things are not going well; when things are bad. And in most educational systems, in most governments, in most societies, in most political movements, in most religions, things are not going well these days.

This is why the world is today the way it is.

The introduction to *CWG - Book 2* says: "We seem to be singularly unable to change ourselves. In spite of what we experience to be not good for us at all, we appear profoundly impotent in the face of the most exciting opportunities to move to new understandings, and remarkably lacking in the strength or the will to do anything within the framework of human affairs other than what we have done before. In short, we keep repeating behaviors, and failed behaviors at that, instead of inventing new ones. We are banging ourselves over the head with a hammer, and we appear to be unable to stop. In this we display lamentable ignorance. We are, as God points out in this book, rather primitive beings."

A look at the newspaper headlines during the time this is being written (mid-April, 1996) offers a remarkable glimpse at the behaviors into which the human race for centuries has fallen, and from which it cannot seem to extricate itself to this very day:

ISRAELI BARRAGE HITS U.N. CAMP IN LEBANON

**MILITANTS IN EGYPT KILL
18 TOURISTS NEAR PYRAMIDS**

**BILL SEEKS TO PROTECT INMATES
FROM GUARDS WHO SEEK SEX**

**CHECHNYA WAR AS FIERCE AS EVER
DESPITE YELTSIN'S PLEDGE**

Seeing their adult role models acting like children, the children of this society begin to act like adults. . .

VERY YOUNG SUSPECTS

> Three boys, two-eight-year olds and one six-year-old, have been arrested near San Francisco on suspicion of attempted murder.
>
> Police in Richmond, California, believe the trio brutally kicked and beat a month-old baby they found in a house from which they were stealing a bicycle. The baby was in critical condition with severe head injuries. His parents were at work and a sister was in another part of the house during the attack.
>
> The suspects were caught with the stolen bicycle after being reported by witnesses. They're being held at a juvenile hall. Authorities are trying to decide how to handle the case.
>
> – *Reuters New Service, 4/24/96*

While such evidences startle and disturb us, the effect is generally momentary. The human race shakes its collective head and moves on, offering very little and doing very little to encourage, stimulate, or produce (much less demand) any real behavioral change. Only a tiny handful of humans is actually engaged in any ongoing effort to free our race from the agonies of its own device.

The *Conversations with God* trilogy is crucial to that effort. *Book 1* of that trilogy explores questions basic to the individual human experience, and gently points the way to sanity. *Book 2* examines our present circumstance as a planetary community, and offers blueprints for change. *Book 3* provides insights into the universal cosmology, describes how life is lived in more advanced civilizations elsewhere, and issues a clarion call to those who would seek a newer world.

Taken together, the trilogy amounts to an extraordinary invitation to create and participate in the most sweeping social, sexual, political, economic, and spiritual revolution in the history of the Earth.

This guidebook is part of that invitation. It takes you step by step through the amazing information in *Book 1*, directing you always to your experience of what is true. For it is now clear that the reason we as a race continue to exhibit and repeat old behaviors is that we have not given ourselves permission to stop listening to old instructions.

Just as our children, sadly, emulate us, so have we emulated our own forebearers, living as they have told us to live, believing what they have told us to believe, adopting the values they have told us to adopt.

These are the values that are killing us. And we will *not* extricate ourselves from the traps of our own devise unless and until we can find a way to move into our *experience* of life, rather than what we have allowed others to tell us must be true.

That is why this guidebook places so much importance on your experience, and why it seeks to render the wisdom in *Conversations with God - Book 1* functional, rather than observational or referential.

If the invitation which the *CWG Trilogy* represents – an invitation to change the whole of the human experience – seems a bit grandiose to you, understand that what we are talking about here is a change in *your* experience. For what has been said so many times is true: the human revolution begins with you.

As you shift and change your own experience, the experience of the whole human race begins to shift and change as well. So this is important work you are doing, this business of changing your life. It has larger consequences than those of which you may initially have been aware.

The guidebook you are holding seeks to assist you in moving the wisdom you found in *Conversations with God - Book 1* into your life as *personal experience.*

The Part You Play in This Book

In order for this book to be experiential, you will have to allow it to be. You will need to be willing to play a part in the book's unfoldment. In a sense, you could choose to be its co-author, just as I chose to be the co-author of *CWG.*

If you make that choice you will answer the inquiries, do the exercises, and undertake the assignments and experiments in this guidebook. By this means you will add to the book something which no one else can add. And you will write its ending yourself. That ending will be found on the pages of your own life story.

You do not have to do the exercises, of course. You may skip the assignments as well. This guidebook will still have great value for you even if you do nothing but read it.

So by all means read it, whether you intend to do the exercises and assignments or not. Simply notice the extent to which you are willing to go. Notice the investment you are willing to make. Then make it, in a way and at a level which is comfortable for you.

Are you willing to spend the time to truly study CWG? What do you think you would get out of it if you did?

How This Guidebook is Organized

More than anything, *Conversations with God - Book 1* is a collection of concepts. It is written in somewhat of a circular fashion, returning the reader over and over again to a set of basic conceptual statements which form the framework of its message. As the person through whom this material came, I did not intend to produce such a construction. That is, I did not do it deliberately. It "just happened" to be the way the questions and answers rolled out. Yet I am clear now that the book's True Author knew exactly what She was doing. I see that not only were His answers inspired, so were my questions. By this device did my Friend produce exactly what was intended: a book embracing the largest spiritual concepts, yet producing the smallest amount of confusion. Circling back over statements which introduced enormous truths, and placing them in new contexts from chapter to chapter, was a wonderful way to do that.

It turns out that God is a good writer.

Each of the chapters in this guidebook covers the major concepts introduced in the corresponding chapter of *Conversations with God - Book 1*. Thus, one can move front to back through the *CWG* text and, whenever a new concept is introduced, turn to the corresponding chapter here and find an opportunity to both explore that concept in greater depth, and render it functional in one's daily life.

Some of the chapters in this book are divided into sections, owing to the fact that the corresponding chapter in *CWG* contained so much information that it would have been very difficult to take it in "one gulp."

CWG's Chapter 1, for instance, is the longest chapter in the book, and any fruitful study of it would have to be done in sections, taking a small portion of the content at a particular sitting. The same is true of several later chapters.

The Guidebook also indicates where to stop your study for the moment and give yourself time to pause and reflect, work on an assignment, or even conduct an experiment to see how – and whether – the text relates to you.

You will see this sign. . .

to pause and reflect

. . .where those stops should be made. Each "stop" sign marks the ending of a class or individual study session. Gliding past these natural stopping points to move through the Guidebook more quickly could lead to misunderstanding – or simply missing – a point the book is trying to make. Don't go too fast. Give yourself some time.

The Conceptual Framework of CWG

The concepts in *Book 1* are extraordinary and breathtaking. Some are simple, some are complex. All are incisive, cutting to the core of the human experience, striking at the heart of our human belief systems, and driving right to the point of human life itself.

There are 34 core concepts around which the book's message revolves.

1. God is communicating with us all the time.
2. Feeling is the language of the Soul.
3. Thought, Word and Deed are the three levels of creation.
4. There are only two Sponsoring Thoughts: fear and love.
5. In the absence of that which you are not, that which you are. . .is not.
6. There is no such thing as "Right" and "Wrong."
7. What you fear, you attract.

8. God is Life, and the Stuff Life Is.
9. God needs nothing, and therefore requires nothing from us.
10. God talks to everyone.
11. Human beings consist of three distinct energies.
12. All you see in your world is the outcome of your idea about it.
13. All conditions are temporary. Nothing stays the same. Which way a thing changes depends on you.
14. The purpose of the soul is evolution.
15. You are who you think you are. You are your own thoughts about yourself, made manifest.
16. Life is not a process of discovery, it is a process of creation.
17. God commands no one.
18. What you resist persists.
19. Passion is not expectation, and expectation is not passion.
20. Suffering is not necessary
21. You need no God.
22. All relationship is holy.
23. Your purpose in life is to decide and to declare, to express and to experience Who You Really Are; this is the purpose of ALL of life; that is evolution.
24. Relationships work best when you always do what is best for you.
25. You are a messenger.
26. You are the truth.
27. God's love is unconditional.
28. There's enough.
29. You are a human being.
30. To want something is to push it away from you.
31. Your life is not about your body
32. Your health is your creation.
33. You are part of the body of God.
34. All of life is a conversation with God.

Understanding these concepts requires deep thought. Functionalizing them, putting them into action, requires deep commitment. Commitment to their truth, commitment to oneself, commitment to the purpose of life.

The purpose of life is to know yourself, create yourself, experience yourself as Who You Really Are. There is no other reason to do anything.

You are doing this right now, and every day of your life. Your every thought, your every word, your every action is a statement to the Universe: *This is Who I Am.*

Most of you are making that statement unconsciously; that is, without thinking. I mean that literally. You are deciding, creating, and experiencing Who You Are *without thinking.* Yours is therefore a thoughtless creation. You have given it no thought whatsoever.

This may seem a harsh indictment. Yet if you look at your life honestly, you will see that it is at least to some degree true. Most of you spend much of your life sleepwalking. You are "on automatic." You go from place to place, move from function to function, slide from utterance to utterance, without conscious thought. You say things without thinking, do things without thinking, and actually *think things without thinking.* (That is, you are not thinking about what you are thinking about.)

Yet there is one thought you do have about all of this – and that is the most dangerous thought of all.

You think none of this makes any difference.

All of this, of course, is why your life is the way it is.

This Guidebook could change all of that.

Let us now look at *Conversations with God - Book I* concept by concept, and see how we can make this wisdom useful in our daily lives. For if wisdom isn't useful, of what use is it?

How You May Want To Proceed If You Are In A Study Group

If you are a member of a *CWG* study group, here are some suggestions on how you may wish to create each study session.

1. Begin each study group session with a brief meditation. Call forth clarity and understanding as your experience.
2. Take a moment for check-in – a very brief statement from each person, moving quickly around the group, to say in a word or two how it goes with them. But remember, this is not a "therapy" group, so resist mightily the temptation to "get into people's stories." *(HINT: You may actually want to form a mutual support group of people willing to meet after the study group – or on another night – for the purpose of dealing with individual emotional issues, rather than studying* CWG.*)*

3. After check-in, move through the group for a 15-20 minute review of the results of last week's assignment or experiment. This is often an important time of sharing and mutual discovery.

4. A short break is often best placed after item 3.

5. Begin this week's study material by having a member of the study group read aloud from the narrative which begins the chapter of this guidebook. When you get to the Exercise, read the directions aloud and then give the group 5 or 10 minutes to complete the process.

6. Discussion of the Exercise and how it was experienced by members of the group. An important time of sharing and discovery.

7. Select another person from the group and continue reading aloud from the narrative material which follows the Exercise in the guidebook.

8. At the end of the chapter, read aloud and discuss the coming week's assignment or experiment. Make sure everyone understands it and that there are no questions.

9. Conclude the study session with a clearing process, making sure that no one is "hanging out" with "unfinished business" as a result of the evening's work. This is the "good-bye check-in" to make sure everyone is all right.

10. A brief (that's a key word here) closing meditation.

Contents

Chapter 1

God Never Shuts Up

I believe the charm and the wonder of *Conversations with God* is that it contains so many mind-expanding, paradigm-shifting, belief-challenging statements, yet has found a way to place these statements before us in a manner which is non-offensive, and even inviting.

The book opens, for instance, with what for some has long seemed a heresy: an announcement that God has never stopped talking to us.

As it happens, an enormous number of people believe God *has* stopped talking, and that He did so many, many years ago. These people believe that God hasn't said a word since. Not in Direct Revelation, at any rate. His full and final word, they say, is found in the Scriptures.

What scriptures? Well, now that depends upon to whom one is speaking. Many say, the Bible. Others say, no, His word is found in the Hebrew Bible. Others say, no, His word is found in the Koran.

Others say, no, it's in the Torah.
Others say, no, in the Mishna.
Others say, the Talmud.
Others, the Bhagavadgita.
Others, the Rig Veda.
Others, the Brahmanas.
Others, the Upanishads.
Others, the Mahabharata and the Ramayana.
Others, the Puranas.
Others, the Tantras.
Others, the Tao-te Ching.
Others, the Buddha-Dharma.
Others, the Dhammapada.
Others, The Master of Huai-nan.
Others, the Shih-chi.

Others, the Pali Canon.
Others, the Book of Mormon.
Others. . .

Well, the point is, many people believe that Direct Revelation – that is, God speaking directly to mankind – has not occurred since the Holy Scriptures (with which they feel comfortable) were written.

And while few of those who cite these sources agree with each other theologically, many agree on one thing emphatically: *their* Word of God is THE Word of God; *their* way to paradise is THE way to paradise; *their* communication from Deity is THE communication from Deity.

By this measure, *Conversations with God* would have to be heresy; would by definition be blasphemy. Some of the adherents of the Old Books may not be clear about *which* old book contains the Truth, but they *are* clear that no *new book* does.

Surprisingly, even some of the newer, more theologically liberal movements deny even the *possibility* that God could be delivering new truth to anyone today through direct communication, and warn against such latter-day revelations.

And so, at its very beginning (indeed, by its very title) *Conversations with God* presents a challenge, upsets the apple cart, turns most present-day theology on its ear. Yet, interestingly, few people seem to have minded; few who have read *CWG* seem to have any quarrel with the possibility, at least, that God has revealed Himself once more through the written word.

Indeed, I'll go further. An astonishing number of people have come forward to say that *they, too, have experienced such communications*. And so it turns out that my conversation with God may not be such an "uncommon dialogue" after all.

Let's explore this opening thought and see how it relates to you.

The first major concept in *CWG* is that God is communicating with us all of the time; has *always* been communicating with us; has never *stopped* communicating with us; and will use whatever tool is at hand to *continue* that communication, both now and even forever more.

TEXT REFERENCE:

I talk to everyone. All the time. The question is not to whom do I talk, but who listens? *– page 3*

This, then, is our starting point in this experiential guide.

CONCEPT #1
God is communicating with us all the time.

Let's now see if this is true for you. Let's look to your experience. Has there ever been a time when *you* felt *inspired by God?* Think about this. What would that look like? How would that feel? Is it possible that you have been touched by such inspiration and didn't even know it? Could it be that you have had just such an experience, and simply *haven't called it that?*

I remember an evening several years ago when I was having dinner with a lady friend at her home. A knock came at the door and it was my lady friend's sister, bursting in to announce that she was going to commit suicide. She was serious too. I talked her out of it.

It wasn't easy. It took most of the evening. I listened carefully, I talked a bit, I listened some more, I talked some more. When our dialogue was over and the sister had gone to the bathroom to wash her face and fix her makeup, my lady friend looked at me with astonished gratitude. "How did you know what to *say*?" she asked.

"I don't know," I remember replying. "I don't even know now what I *did* say."

Today I would answer that question differently. Today I would say, "God gave me the words. God spoke directly to your sister, through me."

I am willing to wager that most people can remember times when God spoke or acted through them. They may not have labeled it that, but they have definitely had the experience.

When my son Travis was around seven or eight, we shared an interesting experience. The family was at dinner when Travis suddenly jumped from the table and began racing around the house, his arms waving, his hands shaking wildly, his face covered with panic.

"What's the matter?" I shouted, but I immediately knew the answer. *"Are you choking?"*

He flashed a look at me I will never forget. It not only said "Yes, *Yes!*" it also said, "Help me! DO SOMETHING."

Cursing myself for not having taken the Red Cross short course and learned the Heimlich Maneuver, I ran to him, put my left arm around his chest, held him in place and slammed the middle of his upper back with the palm of my hand. I don't know what I thought I was doing. Dislodging something, I hoped.

It didn't work. Travis was shaking more violently, convulsing with lack of oxygen. His eyes, popping out now, again pierced through me with a message from deep inside his soul: YOU ARE MY ONLY HOPE.

I knew time was running out.

Now I am not a very big person, not a very strong person as men go. I've always been on the slight side, and I have never acquired much muscle. So I don't know how I got it into my head that I could even do what I did next.

Bending down and reaching for his ankles, I lifted Travis high into the air by his two feet, and held him there with *one hand.* Dangling him upside-down, I again thumped his back, this time quite hard, using the meat of my palm. Nothing. I did it again, *very* hard.

(It's not easy to hit your own child that way. You can never know how difficult until you have to do it. I remember thinking, "a bruise is better than death.")

There was a *gawk!* sound, and something – a huge chunk of some damned thing – popped out of Travis' mouth and flew across the room. I put my son down. He gasped for air. He was breathing again.

"Never mind," I heard my partner telling 911, "It's okay. Everything's all right."

I realized as I looked at my son that I could have lost him. Right then. Right there. The other boys were at the table. "Yea, Dad!" they cheered. "Are you all right?" I asked Travis. "Yeah," he replied weakly. "Excuse me," I said, and went upstairs to my bedroom. I sat on the bed and cried.

Thank you, God. God, thank you for showing me the way. For giving me the strength. . .

Many of us have experienced moments such as this, moments in which we became a larger version of ourselves. I am convinced that in these moments God is talking to us; God is communicating with us; God is acting through us, showing us the way.

The first step in understanding that God is communicating with us *always* is knowing that God is communicating with us *sometimes.* If you can accept the latter, you can begin to see the possibility of the former.

EXERCISE

Remember a time when you were "larger" than your Self; when you did something you didn't know you could do, or said something you didn't know you had it in you to say.

This doesn't have to be something Earth-shattering, like saving someone's life, or announcing the cure for cancer. It can be something as simple as solving a problem with which you or another has been beset, uttering a single sentence that suddenly makes things clear to someone who has been trapped in confusion, or coming up with a really good idea just when you needed one.

If you have had more than one such experience, pick the most striking one; the one which made the biggest impression on you. Share this now in your group — or, if you are doing this exercise alone, write this down in your Guidebook journal — answering the following questions:

What happened which "triggered" your move to a "larger space"?
What did you say or do that was "larger" than the "usual you"?
What did you feel when the experience was over?
What did you come to know or decide about yourself as a result?

Most people have experienced at least one such time in their life. If you cannot think of a single time in which you "showed up" larger than yourself, ask yourself the following questions, giving the group your answers, or placing them in your journal.

1. What would it take for me to consider something I have said or done as something very special?
2. Is there anything I have ever done in my life which could fall into that category?
3. What stops me from being able to acknowledge myself for this?
4. Does self-acknowledgment of something special which I have done make my having done it "less special"?
5. Does God want us to be special? Is it okay to *say so* when we are?

Further discussion: *Spiritual vs. 'Practical' Communication from God*

Have you ever been walking down the street, and for no reason at all found yourself "covered with a feeling" which you could only describe as a "warning" — as if someone inside your head was shouting "look out!"? And have you ever had the experience, in that moment, of looking to your left or your right, only to see a truck coming, or an object falling, or some impending danger looming?

If you have, then you have experienced God talking to you.

Have you ever taken a test, or been given a "pop quiz," or been asked a question, on something you didn't think you knew – only to find the answer mysteriously on the tip of your tongue?

If you have, then you have experienced God talking to you.

Have you ever been deeply hurt, emotionally scarred or wounded, and cried out for an end to the pain, and found yourself in the next instant immersed in a pool of calm, peaceful serenity?

Have you ever been frightened – truly scared – and asked for protection, then to suddenly and almost magically feel impervious to harm, filled with the strength and courage to walk through any experience?

Have you ever faced an incredible dilemma, not knowing the "right" thing to do, only to find that as soon as you let go of your desperate mental struggle, the "right" course of action became immediately apparent to you?

If you have, then you have experienced God talking to you.

Perhaps you can accept that God does "talk" with us, or help us, along the way (or at least that God sends us "guardian angels" or "guides" who do so). Still, the concept of a God who speaks *directly to you* (much less *through you*) on theological matters may be a bit removed from your reality.

Yet if you can accept the former, how can you eliminate the latter? By what manner or means have you come to the determination that God will speak to you of day-to-day things, but not of theological things? Where have you gotten the idea that God suddenly shuts up when the questions get tough? Is it your thought that, while you may be worthy of a warning about a car careening around the corner, you are not worthy of being told the highest truths and the deepest secrets of the universe? And by what measure have you arrived at this assessment of your unworthiness?

> *Is it possible that clearing illness out of the body is okay for God to do, but clearing confusion out of the mind is not?*

Remarkably (and regrettably), many have come to it through organized religion. It is one of life's saddest ironies that the very institutions which are intended to bring us closer to God often push us further away.

Perhaps the most striking paradox of many organized religions is that they ask you to believe in a God Who may be called upon at any time to help you meet life's most difficult challenges – but Who may not be called upon to help you answer life's most difficult questions.

Indeed, if you are asked where you come up with the answers to the difficult spiritual questions which confront you, and you should reply, "Why, I receive all of my answers directly from God. God speaks to me directly," you might well be called a blasphemer. (That is, unless the people to whom you reveal this agree with the answers you have been "given" – in which case you may be called a prophet.)

Most religions ask you to accept their truth, not your own. In this I believe that most religions err. It has been made clear to me that in life the biggest choice you will ever make is the choice between your truth and the truth of another.

to pause and reflect

EXPERIMENT

Look to see how many times God is communicating with you this week.

Buy a small, pocket-sized spiral notebook. Use it to make a daily "log" of the communications you are receiving from God. Do not judge yourself in this. Do not tell yourself this "can't be happening" to you, or that it "isn't what it seems." Simply notice every time you feel you are receiving a communication from a higher source. Take out the notepad and mark down the date and the time.

Then relate in a few words the "message" you have received. Make a note of the form in which the message came to you. Was it a thought without pictures? Was it a picture in your mind? Was it something outside of your mind, in your exterior world? A magazine article which just "fell into your lap"? A song you heard, a movie you saw? Was it something someone said, at just the right moment, in just the right way? Was it a feeling which swept over you? Describe the form in which the message came.

Look to see if there is any increase in the number of these "messages" from the beginning of the week to the end. (Often, noticing the first few causes you to notice many more.)

When the week has passed, and you've completed your list, look over the entries, asking yourself these questions:

Do you believe these communications came directly from God? Do you think you are worthy to receive such communications?

Can you feel any difference between communications which seem to be coming from a higher source, and other thoughts and ideas which move through your head, or experiences which come to you? If so, how would you describe this difference?

What, if anything, does this tell you about life, and your conversations with God?

Chapter 1, Section 2

. . .and nothing but the Truth, so help you God

In life, the biggest choice you will ever make is the choice between your truth and the truth of another.

And how can you know which truth is "truly" yours? *Conversations with God* says by listening to what you are feeling. Feelings reside in the soul, and the soul is God-in-you. In this place is your truth, and it is in no other.

CONCEPT #2
Feeling is the language of the Soul.

Most of our adult lives are spent learning to trust our feelings. This is not surprising, since most of our growing up years were spent learning to *ignore* them.

Many people were told as children that feelings were not "good." It was not "good" to be angry and to show it. It was not "good" to feel jealous and to show it. It was not "good" to feel scared and to show it. It was not "good" even to feel too excited and to show it. It was not good, it was not good, it was *not good.*

If we ran into a room filled from head to toe with youthful exuberance, we were told to hold it down, to not interrupt, to keep still. If we stormed away hurt and angry, we were told to stop that right now, apologize this instant, never speak to elders that way again. If we laughed too loud or cried too long, spoke too soon or asked too much, we were made to know that we had somehow done something "wrong." We had not been "good."

In all of this, we couldn't have missed the point; we couldn't have escaped the message. Life wasn't about learning how to *be*, it was about learning how *not* to be, what we were.

For many adults the biggest challenge is to remember Who They Really Are. Such a big portion of them has been dropped by the wayside, left behind, abandoned, stifled, ignored.

Do you want to know who you are? Do you want to get back in touch with your truth about things – whatever those things may be? Then check out your feelings. Listen to your Soul.

TEXT REFERENCE:

If you want to know what's true for you about something, look to how you're feeling about it. – *page 3.*

EXERCISE

Look to see what you are "feeling" right now about this book and what it is saying. Discuss this in your group, asking each person to describe their feeling about the material you are now reading. If you are working alone, write this in your Guidebook journal.

If you have completed this, go on.

Remember the last time you felt strongly about something. Anything. It doesn't matter. Just remember the last time you felt really strongly about something.

Bring this moment to your mind. Remember the incident; remember the experience; try to remember the exact feeling. Then answer the following questions.

Were your feelings expressed to others at the time?

If so, how did you feel after expressing your feelings?

If they were not expressed, why were they withheld?

How did you feel after withholding them?

How do you feel today about expressing to others what is going on with you?

	Really Okay About It	A Little Ill At Ease	Very Uncomfortable
When I express my deepest feelings to others, I am	☐	☐	☐
When I keep things to myself, I am	☐	☐	☐
When others express their deepest feelings to me, I am	☐	☐	☐

Further discussion: *Feelings vs. emotions*

Try not to confuse feelings with emotions.

Your feelings are what you know about a thing. Your emotions are what you do with what you know.

A feeling is energy.

An emotion is energy in motion.

There is a difference between the two.

Your feeling is your truth. It is exactly how you feel about a thing, based on what you factually and intuitively know.

Because feelings are what you know about a thing, they will always be your truth, but they may not be *the* truth. That is, they may not be what you would have formerly called Objective Truth, especially if you look only at what you factually know, and set aside or ignore what you intuitively know.

There is no such thing as Objective or Factual Truth in this Reality. All truth in our world is created by the context within which it is experienced or observed.

Within the context of your life, for instance, the Sun is "up," the Earth is "down," the air and the sky are between. To Neil Armstrong, on his way to the Moon, there were, no doubt, many moments when the sun wasn't "up" at all, but "down." He may have found himself looking "up" at the Earth instead. Up and down are relative terms. We can all understand this. What we don't understand (or perhaps simply don't want to confront or deal with) is that *all* of "reality" is relative – which is to say that all truth is contextual. . .which is to say that nothing is *truly* true at all!

Still, to make some sense out of our lives, to put some order into them, we *decide upon* what we choose to call Objective Truth.

> *Can you explain the difference between feelings and emotions?*

If, therefore, what you know about a thing is false, or incomplete, or misleading (within the context of your planet's self-created Objective Truth), you will have a false, or incomplete, or misleading "feeling." This will make it no less your *truth*. You will still "truly feel that way." Your feelings will simply not be what is Objectively True within the larger context of your life.

When I was around 8 or 9, I once thought I was drowning as a result of a childhood prank played on me by another boy my age. It was both a frightening and an embarrassing experience, because I was mocked and jeered by my older brother and his friends for not realizing that the "crisis" in which I found myself could have been resolved by my simply standing up, instead of flailing around. It turns out the water in which I'd been dumped was only three feet deep!

Years later, as an adult, I was desperately afraid to go near the water – would not even venture into the deep end of a swimming pool – out of fear that I would drown.

This is an instance in which what I "knew" about a thing (namely, "all bodies of water are unsafe; you are going to drown") was, within the context of life as I was then living it, "false," or incomplete, or misleading. That made it no less my truth. *I truly felt that way!* Yet Objective Truth within the larger context of my life was that the pool, at the edge of which I stood utterly paralyzed, was not even as deep as I was tall; that there were two lifeguards within 50 feet of me; and that the place was full of people who were obviously competent swimmers – one of which was my own wife, gently urging me to get over my fear and get into the water.

The Objective Truth within the context of my world at that moment was that I was clearly not very likely to drown if I slipped into the deep end of this pool. Yet do you think that allowed me to do it? *Not on your life.*

Now just about the time I was getting in touch with these feelings, someone in my party came over to me and made fun of my fear, grabbing me and pulling me toward the edge of the pool, playfully threatening to throw me in. I turned and let out a stream of invectives which shattered the poolside merriment of that Sunday afternoon and embarrassed my wife to high heaven.

I had given in to my emotion.

Emotion is the power which creates, but it has nothing to do with what is really so. (Little of what you create in your life does.)

Emotion is neither true nor false. It is simply energy in motion, and so, it simply *is*.

An emotion is an experience. A feeling is a *knowing*.

How you *feel* is what you *know* about a thing. How you *express* those feelings is how you *emote* – or experience *emotion*. That is, how you place *energy into motion*.

TEXT REFERENCE:

Emotion is energy in motion. When you move energy, you create effect. – ***page 54.***

You do not have to place energy into motion around any feeling. To do or not to do this is your choice. Many people do not know this. They confuse feelings with emotion, and imagine that because they *know* something, they *must do something about it.* That is, they must set energy into motion. And so they have an *emotional response* to a thing. They have added emotion (energy moving) to a feeling (a knowing). This can produce all manner of interesting results.

You can *know* (feel) that you love a person, but you don't have to *do anything about it.* You can *know* (feel) that you dislike a person, but you don't have to *do anything about it.* It is when you translate what you *know* (what you are feeling) into *action* (e+motion=energy in motion) that you have an "emotional response." This is not to say that an emotional response is bad. As a matter of fact, the term "bad" is totally out of place here, for there is nothing that is "good" *or* "bad." There is only that which *serves your purpose* – or does not.

Your Purpose (and that word is capitalized deliberately to underline its importance) is the key to everything. In order to know whether anything (including an "emotional reaction") serves your Purpose, you have to know what your Purpose *is.* If you are not clear as to your Purpose in any given moment or situation, to say nothing of all of life, it will be very difficult for you to decide or to choose how you want to act or react; which is to say, how you want to *be.*

Beingness is everything. And so this decision, this choice, is no small matter.

Many people believe that this business of "beingness" is not a choice; that we are being what we are being, and we can't help it; that we are reacting the way we are reacting, and we can't help it; that we are simply "having an emotional reaction," and what's wrong with that?

There's nothing wrong with it, of course, as it has just been pointed out. Ah, but whether it *serves* you. . .that's another matter.

Further discussion: ***Listening to feelings when making decisions***

If feelings are the language of the soul, it makes sense that we would do well to listen to our feelings when making decisions. Yet we must be careful not to listen to our *data* and *call* them our feelings. Data resides in the mind. Feelings are the language of the soul. Data is not a feeling. It is a piece of information. (It is not a fluke that the "feeling-less" robot on *Star Trek - The Next Generation* was named "Data.")

When we listen to *data* (i.e., all that we think we "know" about a thing, based on previous experience), we often make one kind of choice. When we listen to *feelings,* we often make another. "Fear" is an *emotion* based on data originating in the mind. Love is a *feeling* based on beingness originating in the soul.

The messages of the Soul are received with ultimate clarity only when we have *moved in consciousness* directly to the soul level, bypassing the mind and all the considerations of the mind, to experience the truth of our Being. (That is, the truth of what we are now *being.*)

EXERCISE

List your last three *major* decisions. Use the forms to analyze them.

My last three **major** decisions:

1. On ____________________ I decided to ____________________
Give date or year
____.

2. On ____________________ I decided to ____________________
Give date or year
____.

3. On ____________________ I decided to ____________________
Give date or year
____.

Why I made these decisions:

1. I made decision #1 because ____________________
____.

2. I made decision #2 because ____________________
____.

3. I made decision #3 because ____________________
____.

Looking back, I see that these were decisions of the . . .

	Mind	Soul
Decision #1	☐	☐
Decision #2	☐	☐
Decision #3	☐	☐

% of Mind /Soul Decisions

	33%	66%	100%
MIND	☐	☐	☐
SOUL	☐	☐	☐

What, if anything, does this tell you about yourself? Do you think this % would hold up over your last ten important decisions?

Outcome Analysis

How I hoped things would work out. . .	How things actually worked out . . .
Decision #1	
Decision #2	
Decision #3	

Further discussion: *How to tell "what's what"*

The above exercise may have made one thing clear to you: it is not always easy to know "where you're coming from" in making your decisions and choices. Are you listening to the voice in your head? Or, are you following the urgings of your soul?

To differentiate, remember this: what your mind knows is what you factually know. It is your "data." What your soul knows is what you factually *and intuitively* know. (And, indeed, your intuitive information may be much more complete than your factual information.) From this total awareness your *feeling* emerges.

Still, there are those who will tell you that even "intuition" has sometimes fooled them. And they would be right. This is a very delicate thing, this conversation with God. Even within the realm of what seems like "intuition" we receive messages that can sometimes lead to error.

How, then, to know? What, then, to do? Who, then, to "listen to"? Let's see what the text of *CWG* says on this.

TEXT REFERENCE:

The challenge is one of discernment. The difficulty is knowing the difference between messages from God and data from other sources. Discrimination is a simple matter with the application of a basic rule.

Mine is always your Highest Thought, your Clearest Word, your Grandest Feeling. Anything less is from another source. — *page 4*

We have been saying "be out of your mind!" Yet now we speak of your "highest thought." This brings us to a complex question. Are thought and mind the same?

to pause and reflect

ASSIGNMENT:

Look to see how you are making your decisions and choices NOW. *Chances are you will make at least one fairly important decision during the next week. Maybe you are facing an important personal choice right now. Use the forms below to track "where you are coming from" and how you are making present-day decisions and choices. The first form is for a "right now" choice you are facing. The second is for use over the next week. It is a "choice diary."*

Right now a choice I am facing is . . .

____

____

____

When I come from my Mind (prior data) about this choice, here is what I get. . .

____

____

____

When I come from my Soul (intuitive feelings) about this choice, here is what I get. . .

____

____

____

Looking at this I see that between the two there is:

☐ No Difference ☐ A Little Difference ☐ A Big Difference

Here is the difference I see:

MIND	SOUL

This Week I will have the opportunity to make at least one or two important decisions or choices. While I cannot know now on which day those opportunities will fall, I will keep the following "diary" showing the day, and the "place" I experienced myself to be "coming from," when the decision or choice was made.

NOTE: If you are using this Guidebook with a group or class, please bring this assignment with you for discussion.

MONDAY

A choice or decision I had to make today:

Where I "came from" when I made it:

☐ MIND ☐ SOUL

TUESDAY

A choice or decision I had to make today:

Where I "came from" when I made it:

☐ MIND ☐ SOUL

WEDNESDAY

A choice or decision I had to make today:

Where I "came from" when I made it:

☐ MIND ☐ SOUL

THURSDAY

A choice or decision I had to make today:

Where I "came from" when I made it:

☐ MIND ☐ SOUL

FRIDAY

A choice or decision I had to make today:

Where I "came from" when I made it:

☐ MIND ☐ SOUL

SATURDAY

A choice or decision I had to make today:

Where I "came from" when I made it:

☐ MIND ☐ SOUL

SUNDAY

A choice or decision I had to make today:

Where I "came from" when I made it:

☐ MIND ☐ SOUL

SUMMARY

I would summarize the findings here as follows:

Chapter 1, Section 3

Please pay it no mind

We have been saying, "be out of your mind!" Yet now we speak of your "highest thought." This brings us to a complex question. Are thought and mind the same?

The answer is no. That is why it can be said that you (your ego – which is your sense of self) must be out of your mind and searching your soul in order to know your Highest Thought.

Your thought is an *action*. The moment you think, you act. You create something. All thought is creative.

Likewise, a word is an *action*. The moment you speak, you act. You create something. All words are creative.

And, of course, deeds are *actions*. The moment you do something, you create something. All doing is creative.

TEXT REFERENCE:

Every prayer — every thought, every statement, every feeling — is creative. – *page 12*

Your thought produces what you *create* with the energy which you are. So, too, does your word. And likewise, your deeds.

It is important to understand this difference between *thought* and *mind*, otherwise you may be tempted to imagine that they are one and the same.

CONCEPT #3

Thought, Word and Deed are the three levels of creation.

The mind does not create, but thought does. It has been said that you create in your mind. And that is true. You create in your mind *with the energy of your thought.*

TEXT REFERENCE:

Thought is pure energy. Every thought you have, have ever had, and ever will have is creative. – *page 54*

Once more then, thoughts, words and deeds are the energies, or levels, of creation. Each level requires a different kind (vibration) of physical energy.

There is not a single person who has not experienced this truth. There are many who do not know they have experienced it. That is because some are creating consciously – with conscious awareness of the process – and some are living life unconsciously.

The key to our level of consciousness is our awareness of our Sponsoring Thought.

EXERCISE

Think of a time when you had a thought about something, and that thought came true. Discuss this in your group, or write a short statement about it below.

I remember a time when I had the following thought. . .

____

____

____

____

. . .then the following events occurred. . .

____

____

____

____

____

Now think of a time when you wished for something very hard, and it came true; or when you visualized something happening for you, then watched it happen to you, just the way you saw it in your Mind.

What did that feel like?

Did you think afterward that your own wish or visualization had something to do with things turning out the way they did?

What do you think today?

Conversations with God *says that thought is creative. Do you believe this? If you do, and if someone asked, "How does thought create?" — what would you answer?*

Write your answer below:

____

____

____

____

____

____

Review pages 91-93 in Conversations with God. *Discuss this material at length in your group. If you are working through this Guidebook alone, read those pages carefully. Then. . .*

to pause and reflect

ASSIGNMENT:

Examine what role, if any, your thought about a thing has played in your life thus far.

Negative and positive outcomes are part of everyday life. All of us can easily come up with a long list of both from our lives. In the boxes below, list just a few on both ends of the scale, then see if you can remember what your thoughts were just before those events occurred.

List the five most recent "negative outcomes" you can remember. (i.e., "I got fired, " "My spouse left me," "I got sick," "I didn't get the job," etc.)

1.____

2. ____

3. ____

4. ____

5. ____

Now look at these items one by one, and see if you can remember – then list – the thoughts which you had before the outcome occurred.

Negative outcome #1: ____

____

The thought I remember having about it ahead of time:

Negative outcome #2: ____

____

The thought I remember having about it ahead of time:

Negative outcome #3: ______________________________

____

The thought I remember having about it ahead of time:

Negative outcome #4: ______________________________

____

The thought I remember having about it ahead of time:

Negative outcome #5: ______________________________

____

The thought I remember having about it ahead of time:

List the five most recent "positive outcomes" you can remember.

1. ______________________________
2. ______________________________
3. ______________________________
4. ______________________________
5. ______________________________

Now let's turn the paradigm around and look at the positive side.

Positive outcome #1: ______________________________

____

The thought I remember having about it ahead of time:

Positive outcome #2: ______________________________

____

The thought I remember having about it ahead of time:

Positive outcome #3: ______________________________

____

The thought I remember having about it ahead of time:

Positive outcome #4: ______________________________

____

The thought I remember having about it ahead of time:

Positive outcome #5. ______________________________

____

The thought I remember having about it ahead of time:

Now, having finished this part of the assignment, explore the following questions. Discuss your answers in the group, and make a few notes on those answers in the space provided below. If you are using this guidebook individually, write your answers below.

QUESTIONS:

1. Which was it easier to remember and make a list of. . .the positive or the negative experiences?

____.

2. What, if anything, does this tell you about yourself?

____

____

____.

3. You listed five experiences in each category. Giving each experience a weight of 20%, what percentage of your negative experiences were preceded by a thought or a fear of negative outcome? ______ *%*

4. What percentage of the positive experiences which you listed were preceded by a thought or a joyful anticipation of positive outcome? ______ *%*

5. Describe the role which "worry" plays in your life.

I worry about things	☐ a lot	☐ a fair amount	☐ once in a while	☐ very little

Please elaborate on your answer, describing when you worry, if ever, and how that experience is for you.

____

____

____

____

____

____

____

6. Describe the role which "joyful anticipation" plays in your life.

I joyfully anticipate things	☐ a lot	☐ a fair amount	☐ once in a while	☐ very little

Please elaborate on your answer, describing when you joyfully anticipate, if ever, and how that experience is for you.

Chapter 1, Section 4
And now, a word from our sponsor. . .

The key to our level of consciousness is our awareness of our Sponsoring Thought. You may be aware of your present-day thoughts about things, but it is highly unlikely that you are aware of the *first* thought you ever had about those things. Yet your first thought may be the most important thought you ever had on any subject, because in all probability it is your currently operating *Sponsoring Thought.* It sponsors, supports, and surrounds every other thought you have on a subject – until it does not.

This concept of Sponsoring Thought was introduced on page 12 of *Conversations with God*. It explains, at last, what people have been asking for years: If thought is creative, and if I change my idea and my thought about a thing, *why do I not see a change in what I am creating*?

As it turns out, it is *not enough to change your latest thought about a thing*. You must first deal with your Sponsoring Thought.

TEXT REFERENCE:

. . .what you must know — and here is the secret — is that always it is the thought behind the thought — what might be called the Sponsoring Thought — that is the controlling thought. – *Page 12*

Your Sponsoring Thought is usually your first thought, the first thought – or certainly the first serious thought – you ever had about a thing. Now the most important thing for you to know about a Sponsoring Thought is that you cannot erase it or delete it. Once a Sponsoring Thought is there, it's there. Yet you can *add* to your Sponsoring Thought. That is, you can *enlarge* it to include *new data.* This Guidebook hopes to lead you to your new data by taking you to your experiences. We are attempting here to enlarge or expand your Sponsoring Thoughts about everything. As you consider your present Sponsoring Thoughts, understand that there are only two kinds or types.

CONCEPT #4
There are only two Sponsoring Thoughts: fear and love.

CWG says that there are only two places from which all thoughts spring. These are the two ends of the Great Polarity – the Alpha and the Omega – which allow the system which we call "relativity" to be. Every human thought, and every human action, is based in either love or fear.

These two energies are clearly defined in *CWG*, so there can be no mistaking them – and thus, no mistaking from which of them our ideas, decisions and actions emerge. The polarity between love and fear forms the basis of the Law of Opposites, which law is obeyed by all of life in the physical realm.

EXERCISE

See if you can find where in *Conversations with God* the energies called Love and Fear are defined. Read the definitions again for greater clarity.

Now, on the table below, expand on these definitions from your own understanding.

FROM MY OWN LIFE I HAVE LEARNED THAT. . .

Fear is the energy which. . .	Love is the energy which. . .

Not only are the actions of individuals based in love or fear, so, too, are decisons affecting business, industry, politics, religion, education, economics, and everything going on in all of society.

Review pages 19-21 in *Conversations with God*. Discuss this material at length in your group. If you are working through this guidebook alone, read those pages carefully. Then. . .

to pause and reflect

ASSIGNMENT:

Pick up a copy of today's newspaper. Select any ten headlines and make an analysis of these stories.

This is an exercise is seeing where the human race is "coming from" in the conduct of its affairs. Don't read just from the front page. Everyone knows that only the "bad" news makes the first page. Scan the paper throughout. Check the business section and the economic news. Take a look at the lifestyles page. Examine the sports news.

What percentage of the stories reflected actions, decisions, choices or opinions based in Fear as CWG and you have defined it, and what percentage was rooted in Love?

Come prepared to discuss this in your next class, or make a note of it in your journal.

Now check any other source you think would be valuable in coming to a wider or broader view of the human experience. Pick up some magazines. See if you can get your hands on a history book. Look to see what percentage of the decisions, choices, actions, and opinions described in those publications fall into the above two categories.

Now take all of the items you felt would be placed in the category of Fear and look at them again. Ask yourself, if Love had been the Sponsoring Thought, what here would have changed; how else could this story have ended? (You will find this particularly fascinating with a history book.)

Make a notation in your journal and, if you are in a study group with others, bring this information to your next session for discussion.

Chapter 1, Section 5
Like what is unlike what you like

The polarity between love and fear forms the basis of the Law of Opposites, which law is obeyed by all of life in the physical realm.

Conversations with God points to this law throughout its pages, explaining that without this law, we could not experience Who We Really Are. Knowing something and experiencing it are two different things. Spirit longed to know itself experientially. Conceptual awareness was not enough. Yet conceptual awareness – pure *knowingness* – is the state of things in the Realm of the Absolute. There is nothing else, save pure Being. Thus, the physical universe was created as a realm within which we might experience ourselves as that which we Really Are through the experiencing of that which we are not.

It is necessary first for us to know ourselves as that which we are *not* in order to experience That Which We Are.

TEXT REFERENCE:

Once in the physical universe, you, My spirit children, could experience what you know of yourself — but first, you had to come to know the opposite. – *page 27*

This is the next major theme tackled in the *CWG* text. The polarity between love and fear is not only defined, its purpose is explained in some detail. Thus, we arrive at. . .

CONCEPT #5
In the absence of that which you are not, that which you are. . .is not.

What is meant here is that in the physical realm, all things exist in holy relationship to each other. All things are defined by what they are not. Or, as the *CWG* text itself puts it, "you cannot know yourself as tall unless and until you become aware of short. You cannot experience the part of you that you call fat unless you also come to know thin. Taken to ultimate logic, you cannot experience yourself as what you Are until you've encountered what you are not."

EXERCISE

Re-read pages 24 through 28 of *Conversations with God.* If you are in a study group, have various members of the group take turns reading this section aloud. If you are studying at home, read the section aloud onto a tape. Play back the tape so that you may hear these words "read back" to you.

[NOTE: Sometimes it is easier to capture the meaning of the more complex passages in CWG by hearing the words, rather than reading them. As an aid in this process, you may wish to know that the entire text of Conversations with God - Book 1 *is on audio tape and is available in most book stores. It may also be ordered from Audio Literature, 370 West San Bruno, San Bruno, CA 94066, Phone: 1-800-383-0174. The questions were read by me, with the* responses *recorded by actors Ed Asner and Ellen Burstyn.]*

Now do the following exercises in your journal, or, if you are in class, have the moderator or facilitator select group members to respond.

1. List several physical aspects of the many "things you are" (big, tall, short, small, light, dark, fast, slow, etc.) — in other words, describe yourself physically. Then, ask youself how you know that.

Do you have a little, round nose. . .or a long, straight nose?
Do you have a strong, square jaw. . .or a gently curving one?
Are your eyes "dark and mysterious". . .or bright and sparkling?

2. Now name three "things you are" which are not physical (compassionate, humorous, creative, patient, kind, etc.). Just list three things you know yourself to be. Then, look to see how you know that. Just think about this for a second.

to pause and reflect

Further discussion: *Why "bad things" happen to "good people"*

One of the hardest things to understand in life is why it has to be the way it is. That is, why so many "bad things" seem to happen to "good people." Yet if you stopped long enough and looked hard enough in the last exercise, you may have begun to see a pattern. A process. A "way things are" which begins to make sense.

There is a principle of metaphysics which is at play here. Briefly stated:

> The moment you declare yourself to be anything, *everything unlike it will come into your life.*

This is the Law of Opposites to which *Conversations with God* refers. To understand this law better, read the "Parable of the Little Soul and the Sun" on pages 33-34 of *CWG*.

The Law states that you cannot "be" a thing in the absence of that thing which you are *not* being. You cannot be "warm" if you have never "been" cold. You cannot "be" up if you have never "been" down. If you declare yourself to be "patient," you can be sure that anything and everything unlike patience will creep into your life. You will be given ample opportunity to know and experience what you've declared yourself to be.

> *Can you think of a time when this Law played its effect in your life? What was your reaction to it?*

Have you ever declared that you were sick and tired of being short of cash, and that "from now on I am going to be *abundant,*" only to observe that you suddenly have more money problems than ever before?

This is the Law of Opposites at work. You can depend on it every time.

Now the "cure" for this condition is not to wish that things would happen differently, but to react differently to the way things are happening. In fact, do not "react" at all, but rather, *create.*

"Reaction" and "creation" are the same word. Only the "c" has gotten confused. When you "c" things correctly, the problem goes away! The act of creation is "c-ing" things rightly. You must "c" *first.* Then you produce *creation* and not *reaction.*

We "react" to a situation when we act as we did once before. We "create" when we behave in a totally new way – as if nothing like this has ever happened before.

This new way of behaving (that is. . ."BE having") is a powerful response. You *respond*, rather than *react*, to what is occurring. You declare your responsibility (that is, your response-*ability!)* in the situation. When you do this, *you* decide how you are going to "have yourself be," rather than be-having in a way which does not speak of Who You Are. . .and who you choose to Be.

Never have a state of "beingness" which you do not choose to have. When you do, you are be-having badly! I suggest that you always be-have nicely. It's a far happier way to live. Still, remember this: Never "should" on yourself.

to pause and reflect

EXPERIMENT

Think of some events that commonly occur in your life to which you generally "react" negatively. Use the chart below.

Now decide *ahead of time* how you are going to "create" the way you choose to "be" the next time these common occurrences take place.

This is an experiment in Conscious Creation.

We've started the list for you to give you some examples.

THINGS WHICH COMMONLY OCCUR	MY USUAL REACTION when these things happen	MY NEW REACTION the next time they happen
Someone cuts me off in traffic		
I've been "ripped off" by an offer to which I sent good money and can't get it back		
My spouse (partner, friend), who is always late, is late again, causing me great inconvenience		

You may want to re-draw this chart on a larger sheet of paper to give you more examples.

Chapter 1, Section 6
Can you believe the promise of God?

Never "should" on yourself.

This is the biggest lesson in Chapter 1 of *Conversations with God.* There is nothing you "have to" be, do, or have in order to "please God." You were not given an opportunity to change certain behaviors in the last experiment because you are "supposed to" change these behaviors. You were given the experiment to show you the *possibilities* of life, not the *demands.*

There *are* no demands in life. Not from God. And, truly, not from anyone.

TEXT REFERENCE:

There are no "shoulds" or "shouldn'ts" in God's world. Do what you want to do. Do what reflects you, what re-presents you as a grander version of your Self. — *page 38*

The concept of free will is a difficult concept for many human beings to grasp. They *say* they believe in a God who has given them "free will," but they do not *really* believe it – and they certainly don't *act* like it.

One of the most challenging ideas in *Conversations with God* is the idea that no matter what we do, God doesn't give a damn. That is meant quite literally. No matter what we do, God doesn't *give a damn.*

ALL HE GIVES ARE BLESSINGS.

And that is because. . .

CONCEPT #6
There is no such thing as "Right" and "Wrong."

Most of our lives we have been taught about an angry God, a retributive God who is going to "get us" if we don't behave (that is, be-*have*. . .that is, have a state of *beingness*) in a way which God approves.

According to *CWG*, this is a false teaching. "I have never set down a 'right' or 'wrong,' a 'do' or a 'don't'," God says in the text. Do you think God means that? Can it be true? What is God's rationale for failing to give us any guidelines at all for how She wants us to live?

EXERCISE

Ask your study group to read pages 38-42 of *CWG* aloud. If you are studying at home, listen to the *CWG* Audio Book or record the section on a tape, then play it back so that you may hear these words "read to you." In your journal or in your group, answer the following questions.

(If you are studying alone, please be *sure* to answer these questions *in writing* in your journal. Answering them "in your head" will not be nearly as effective. Trust me. If you are answering these questions out loud in your study group, go home and answer them again tonight in your journal. These may be among the most important questions posed to you in the entire study guide.)

1. How — if in any way at all — would your life have been different if you had come from a "Never should on yourself" philosophy the past 20 years? Would you have changed any of your choices?

2. Are you facing any choices now which this understanding might impact? In what way does it change or affect the options you are considering?

3. Can you think of any way in which this portion of the *CWG* message might change your life in the future?

Further discussion: *What, then, is God's purpose?*

If God has no preference in the matter of how we behave, if God has no restrictions, rules, or regulations by which we may undertake the living of our lives, then what, exactly, is God "up to"? Why has He put us here, and what does She expect from us, anyway? This the thinking mind begs to know. This the human race has pondered from the beginning of time. What is God's ideal? What is God's purpose?

Have you ever feared God? If so, who created in you your first fear of God? *CWG* focuses on this question many times throughout its text. It does so with exquisite articulation on page 43. Read the section beginning, "This is My plan for you. This is My ideal."

Many people do not believe it is possible that God would grant to human beings the gift of real free choice; many find it difficult to accept that God doesn't condemn us, no matter what we do. The paragraphs on the bottom on page 44 of *CWG* offer a gentle, yet powerful, response to this thought. Reading them, we are filled with a great truth. It is time to step away from our fear of God.

to pause and reflect

ASSIGNMENT:

Copy the paragraphs on the bottom of page 44 of CWG *onto a poster and place it on your refrigerator, or on the bathroom mirror – someplace you will see it every day.*

Ponder often the meaning and the message of the final sentence.

Chapter 1, Section 7
My ultimate fear is this. . .

It is time to step away from our fear of God.

What stops us from believing the most wonderful thoughts we ever had about God is, of course, our fear of God. This fear is so great, so powerful, that it has caused us to make God out to be more like a devil than a deity. It is our fear which causes us not only to deny God, but to deny ourselves as Who We Really Are as well.

TEXT REFERENCE:

. . .you have assigned devilish characteristics to God in order to convince yourself not to accept the God-like promises of your Creator, or the God-like qualities of the Self.

Such is the power of fear. – *page 53*

Fear of God produces fear of life itself. And fear of life produces absolute paralysis. Worse, fear can actually produce dreadful outcomes.

CONCEPT #7
What you fear, you attract.

It is without a doubt demonstrably true that what you fear, you attract. What you fear most is what will most plague you. Your fear will draw it to you like a magnet. That is because – as *Conversations with God* explains beginning on page 54 – emotion is the power which attacts, and fear is one of the strongest emotions.

Later in *CWG* is found the following statement: "Fear is the opposite of everything you are, and so has an effect of opposition to your mental and physical health. *Fear is worry magnified* (*CWG*, page 188)." Fear attacks your body at a cellular level. It is impossible to have a healthy body under conditions of continuing fear.

EXERCISE

Are there some things which you have feared in the past which have actually come to pass? What happened when these fears turned to reality? And what does any of that mean to you now?

Do you have any fears in your life right now? What are they? Using the chart below, take a close look at your fears, and what you think would happen if they were realized. Sometimes simply looking closely at the outcomes you fear eliminates much of the fear itself.

Finish this exercise and include your comments about it in your journal. If you are in a study group, have the group stop for a moment and complete the form below.

LOOKING AT PAST FEARS

Three things I have feared in the past which have actually happened are:

1. ______________________________

2. ______________________________

3. ______________________________

An analysis of what occurrred in my life as a result of these fears being realized shows that:

With regard to #1 above, after what I feared came true, my life changed in the following way:	With regard to #2 above, after what I feared came true, my life changed in the following way:	With regard to #3 above, after what I feared came true, my life changed in the following way:

LOOKING AT PAST FEARS

As I look at my life today, I see that I

a. ☐ still have some fears

b. ☐ have pretty much eliminated fear from my experience

If you checked "a", complete the box below. If you checked "b", skip this box.

THREE THINGS I FEAR, AND WHAT I THINK WOULD HAPPEN IF THEY CAME TO PASS:

I am afraid that ____
____.

If this happens, I believe that___________________________________
____.

I am afraid that ____
____.

If this happens, I believe that___________________________________
____.

I am afraid that ____
____.

If this happens, I believe that___________________________________
____.

What, if anything, does the above analysis tell you about your fears? ____
____
____
____
____
____
____

Do you choose to make any decisions with regard to this?

STOP

to pause and reflect

ASSIGNMENT:

Keep a small notebook with you during the next week. Each time you notice yourself moving into fear, or feel apprehension about something, make an entry in the notebook.

Before turning in each night, create and fill out a form like the model below and on the next page. Bring the forms to your study group next week, or to your study session if you are working at home. In the group, or in your journal, share what this process has brought to you.

NIGHTLY FEAR REPORT:

Fill out one form for each entry in your notebook.

Today I noticed that I felt fear or apprehension around the following:

This is what I am afraid might happen:

If that *did* happen, here's what would probably happen next. . .

And if *that* happened, here's what would probably happen next. . .

And if *THAT* happened, here's what would probably happen next. . .

And if THAT HAPPENED, here's what would probably happen next. . .

And if ALL OF THIS HAPPENED, here's what would probably result:

So here is what I am ultimately afraid of. . .

Additional Inquiries
from Chapter 1

In addition to the overarching concepts explored in the main sections of this Guidebook, each chapter of *Conversations with God* contains many specific ideas I feel it is important to be familiar with if one is to have a rich understanding of this material. We therefore conclude each chapter in the Guidebook with a list of Additional Inquiries encouraging deeper exploration.

These questions drive to some of the finer points in the text. The thought and discussions which will result from exploring these questions cannot help but enhance your ability to apply the book's truths to real life, rendering this wisdom functional in your daily experience. That, of course, is the point of it all.

For study groups the questions form a perfect basis for regular interactive dialogues. If you are moving through this Guidebook at home, responding to the questions in writing in your journal will greatly sharpen comprehension.

The answers to the Additional Inquires concluding each chapter are found in the back of this Guidebook. Each answer is followed by a page number in parentheses for your convenience in locating the relevant portion of the text. This answer key may be used by study group leaders to facilitate the group's discussion. For group participants and those working on their own, try not to refer to the answer key or the text until you have attempted to answer the question on your own.

1. CWG lists four methods by which God communicates with us. What are they?
2. How do you know when a communication is from God rather than some other source?
3. Why does God seem to talk to some people, and not others?
4. Asking God for anything is the "wrong" way to pray. Why?
5. Why does it appear that some prayers go unanswered?
6. God is the creator of all things. *True or False?*
7. What are the two great illlusions of man?
8. All human actions are fueled by one of two emotions. They are?
9. What is a Sponsoring Thought?
10. What is the soul's only desire?
11. Why did God create our relative world?
12. Explain the Law of Opposites.

13. Describe the concept of the Holy Trinity in metaphysical terms.
14. What are the three steps in the evolution of humankind?
15. What is the difference between relationships of the gross (i.e. physical) level and relationships of the sublime level?
16. In a parable of the Little Soul and the Sun, why was the soul surrounded by darkness?
17. There is only one reason to do anything. What is it?
18. Are the world's calamities and disasters God's punishment, or simply "bad luck"?
19. What does God want us to do about world starvation, violence, and injustice?
20. To the human soul, what is hell?
21. Does God punish us for our sins?
22. Why didn't Jesus just heal everyone and get it over with?
23. Why does fear attract what is feared?
24. What are the Three Laws of the Universe?

Chapter 2
Who is God?

There are those who say that God is both defineable and describable. Some say that there is no question about it. . .God is a man. Other say, no, God is female. Because most humans are engaged in a constant effort to define themselves, most humans feel it is important to somehow define God. This wouldn't be so bad except that most people also need to believe that *their* definitions of God are the only definitions of God which are *correct.*

Yet God can neither be contained nor defined.

TEXT REFERENCE:

If you think God looks only one way, or sounds only one way or *is* only one way, you're going to look right past Me night and day. — *page 60*

This business of the identity and appearance and message of God has consumed the speculations of human beings everywhere from the beginning of time. Yet the answer to the mystery of who God is, the end of our eternal quest to know God, has been right in front of us all the time. God is. . .*everything.*

CONCEPT #8
God is Life, and the Stuff Life Is.

For many people the above concept is not romantic enough, not holy enough, not religious enough or spiritual enough or, well, *Godly* enough. Yet *Conversations with God* makes it clear that the statement is nevertheless true. Page 60 of the text presents a particularly eloquent pronouncement in this regard.

Now this simple declaration – that God is Everything – has profound implications. For if God is everything, then there is nothing which is *not* God. No human being. No physical object. No experience or emotion. *No thing in our entire universe.*

And this declaration leads to an even more astonishing one. For if no thing in our universe is "not God," then God either judges and condemns a part of Himself, or God judges and condemns no one and nothing.

Could this be possible?

What do *you* think?

EXERCISE

Below is a list of people, emotions, experiences and events.

On a scale of 1 to 10, indicate how much you love (L-1, L-2, L-3, etc.) or condemn (C-1, C-2, C-3, etc.) these things, and then, how much you think God loves or condemns them.

Do not dance away from the second part of this question by saying, "I cannot judge this. Only God can judge." Just make an estimate of how much you ***think*** *God loves or condemns them, based on what you think you know about all of this.*

Person, Emotion, Experience, or Event	How Much I Love Or Condemn This		How Much I Think GOD Loves or Condemns This	
	L	C	L	C
1. Mother Theresa				
2. Beating people up				
3. Raw sex				
4. Genuine love				
5. Adolf Hitler				
6. Earthquakes				
7. Newborn babies				
8. Terminating pregnancy				
9. Jesus Christ				
10. Moses				
11. Krishna				
12. The Buddha				
13. Mickey Mantle				
14. Your father				
15. Compassion				
16. Selfishness				
17. The Holocaust				
18. Peddling drugs to kids				
19. Adults using drugs				
20. You				

Now consider this: Everything you scored under 10 in God's "L" column was an error. Everything you scored over 0 in God's "C" column was an error. God's unconditional love produces God's unconditional acceptance of even our worst "mistakes."

Further discussion: *Does lack of condemnation mean lack of effect?*

Be very careful as you review the exercise above, and the information which precedes it, or it could lead to misunderstanding of how the universe works.

Does God's lack of condemnation mean that our actions – no matter what they are – will produce no negative effect? It does not. By lack of condemnation, God has not eliminated from life the Law of Cause-and-Effect. Everything you do (cause) creates a result (effect). That is the law, and there is no avoiding it.

> *If you felt God was never going to punish you, would it change the way you behave? Would it alter your values? What do your answers to these questions tell you?*

And the effect which you create can reach beyond this particular lifetime. Long after you leave your present body you will feel the effect of all that you have caused. Not as a *punishment*, but simply as a *result*. Unlike punishments or retributions, these results are impersonal. They have nothing to do with you or the "rightness" or "wrongness" of anything you may have done, but merely with what *proceeds as a natural outcome* of what you have done.

If you drop a rock from a building, it will fall to the ground. This will happen not because the rock is "bad," or because dropping it was "wrong," but simply because the Law of Gravity produces that result.

That which is unlike God (Who is Total Love) is a denial of God. This denial of Who You Really Are causes a "falling away." This has nothing to do with punishment. It is a law. It is just what happens. You might call it *spiritual gravity*.

(That may be why, when we do something which is unGod-like, we are often advised by others to "consider the gravity" of what we have done!)

Breaking the law of spiritual "gravity" can produce "grave" results. That is, results which put us in our spiritual grave. We feel as though we are spiritually dead. We feel separated from God. (We can never be truly separated from God, for God is All That Is. Yet we can feel as though we are separated from God.) This is how we "feel about ourselves," and this feeling proceeds from every act which denies Who and What God Is (and thus, who and what We Are).

CWG teaches that the only hell there is, is the feeling of separation from God. This is our spiritual death, for God is life and the stuff life is (the very point and the very concept we are studying in this chapter), and separation from life is felt as "death."

To be enlivened once more, we may have to be "born again" (reincarnated) in order to recreate ourselves anew. Or we may choose to simply remember (that is to say, become once again a member of) Who We Really Are.

to pause and reflect

ASSIGNMENT:

Ask yourself this week, in the quiet of your heart, how can it be possible that God does not condemn anything and anyone? What implications does this have for all humankind?

Chapter 2, Section 2
What good are values?

The striking statements about "right"and "wrong" in *Conversations with God* could cause some people to abandon their personal value systems. Yet *CWG* says you will probably not benefit from doing this.

"Your ideas about right and wrong are just that – ideas," the text asserts. Yet they form the structure of your life, "and to lose them would be to unravel the fabric of your experience."

The book suggests that you may benefit from examining your values one by one. "Do not dismantle the house, but look at each brick, and replace those which appear broken, which no longer support the structure."

If you truly wish to render the wisdom in *Conversations with God* functional in your daily life, take a moment during the next few days and undertake a thorough examination of your present value system. See whether the bricks of the house you have built still support the structure. See whether your values – to which you most often respond automatically, without thinking – are continuing to serve you in every area. If there is an area where a previously held value no longer supports your sense of Who You Are (much less who you Choose To Be), see what it would take to change it, and explore what you think would happen if you did. The forms below are designed to help you do so.

The current values I hold about **money**:

How I experience these values serving me now ____ greatly ____ somewhat ____ not at all

If I altered my values on this, my new idea would be:

I think such change would have the following effect on my life:

The current values I hold about **sex**:

How I experience these values serving me now ____ greatly ____ somewhat ____ not at all

If I altered my values on this, my new idea would be:

I think such change would have the following effect on my life:

The current values I hold about **God**:

How I experience these values serving me now ____ greatly ____ somewhat ____ not at all

If I altered my values on this, my new idea would be:

I think such change would have the following effect on my life:

If you are moving through this material in a study group, you may wish to discuss what these charts reveal to you right now.

Many people have formed their values in certain ways because they believe that God wants them to do so. They hold a thought (usually given to them by others) which says that God needs us to obey His commands, and requires us to do so under penalty of everlasting damnation. The question in the lives of people who hold that thought is not whether their current value system serves *them*, but whether it serves God. Whether they are happy in their lives or not becomes irrelevant. The question is whether God is happy.

People who live within such a paradigm are often deeply threatened when they are told that God is happy no matter *what* you do. The idea that no one and nothing can "make God unhappy" is a foreign one, sounding strange to their ears. More than strange. Blasphemous. For the concept of an unhappy God is central to their theology. The concept of a God Who has needs, and Who becomes so displeased if those needs are not met that He lashes out and punishes us, is at the core of their belief system.

This construction of an angry, jealous, retributive God is held in the thoughts of more people than might be imagined. Yet *CWG* opens the door to a new kind of understanding. It introduces us to a new kind of God. It is a God most of us are grateful to finally meet. As a woman at one of my lectures said, "Thank you for showing me a God I can fall in love with."

And what is so different about this particular God?

CONCEPT #9
God needs nothing, and therefore requires nothing from us.

The question of "right" and "wrong" drives to the heart of a larger inquiry. Does God have needs? For if there is an objective RIGHT and WRONG in the universe, who would have created it? Who would have decided what they should be? And why?

Logic tells us that the only Being in the universe capable of making such choices and conjuring such creations would be God Herself. Yet if God made those decisions, that would seem to indicate that God has a preference in the matter; that God somehow has needs which must be met, or desires which must be fulfilled, and that this is accomplished by the creation of RIGHT and WRONG, and by the commandment by God to His subjects that they had better *do* what is RIGHT and *avoid* what is WRONG, *or else.*

The final paragraph on page 64 of *CWG* says, however, that such demands are counterfeit, having nothing to do with God. "Deity *has* no needs," the text proclaims. "All That Is is exactly that: *all that is.* It therefore wants, or lacks, nothing – by definition."

Yet because God has no needs, and wants nothing, does that mean God has no desires? It does not, for desires and needs are not the same thing – though many people have made them so in their lifetime.

A "need" is something you *must have.* Your happiness, security, peace of mind, etc., depend on it. A desire is something you *choose to have.* It is a *preference.*

One chooses to have a mashed potato rather than a baked potato. One does not need to have this. It is simply a preference. If one were served a baked potato by mistake, one could probably live with it, and actually, in many cases, be perfectly happy (depending upon how attached one is to having one's potatoes mashed).

How about you? Are you clear about the difference between desires and needs? Or do you have these categories confused in your life?

EXERCISE

Let's explore what it takes for you to be happy. This is a chance to see how you've "set it up," how you've constructed it in your reality. In the chart below is a list of the things many people feel they need in order to be happy, safe, and have peace of mind. Check the appropriate column for those things you feel you *need, and those things you simply desire — and could be just as happy without.*

COMMON INGREDIENTS FOR HAPPINESS, SAFETY, AND PEACE OF MIND	NEED IT	DESIRE IT
Someone who loves, in a sexual way, only you		
Challenging & creative work		
A beautiful home		
Lots of sex		
Some kind of work: any job		
Lots of money		
A halfway decent home		
A little bit of sex, for heaven's sake. . .		
At least enough money to pay bills		
The acceptance of others		

In God's world, there are no check marks in the Column marked "NEED IT." How about in yours? Are there any check marks in that column? If so, what would it take to transform these "needs" into "desires" or "preferences"?

Changing what you imagine to be needs into what you experience as desires is the first step on the road to mastery. While Deity has no needs, Deity does have desires. These are outlined on *CWG* page 65.

to pause and reflect

EXPERIMENT

Try moving through the next week of your life operating from a decision that you "need" absolutely nothing; that all of your former "needs" are now merely preferences or desires.

Carry a pocket notebook with you and every time you experience yourself "needing" something during the next week, make an immediate note of it, and write down what would happen to you if you did not get what you think you "need." Make your decision on what to do about meeting your "need" based on this analysis. At the end of the day, write down in what way, if any, this altered your experience.

Report back to the group next week, or make a detailed entry in your *CWG* journal.

Chapter 2, Section 3
You, too, can have a dialogue with God

Over and over again *CWG* makes the assertion that everyone may have a conversation with God. As noted in the introduction to this Guidebook, the text of *CWG* is circular, winding back around to make the same points a number of times.

In its second chapter, the book again addresses the topic with which the entire dialogue opens on page 3 – the matter of to whom God speaks. Please re-read *CWG* from the bottom of page 66 to the middle of page 69. Then, consider this:

CONCEPT #10
God talks to everyone.

Do not go to bed thinking you are "crazy" if you imagine that God has spoken directly to you, or that you are receiving communications directly from God in some other way. If you think you are, you probably are. Do not buy into the world's assessment that you are not "worthy" of hearing from God directly.

TEXT REFERENCE:

This is the root of every problem you experience in your life — for you do not consider yourself worthy enough to be spoken to by God. Good heavens, how can you ever expect to hear My voice if you don't imagine yourself deserving enough to even be spoken to? – *page 69*

It is important, though, to use caution, lest we decide and declare that *every* stray thought which enters our head is a Direct Message from the Divine. *CWG* answers the question of how to differentiate between stray thoughts which come from our ego, and communications from God. Reviewing the bottom of *CWG*, page 4 and the top of page 5 may be helpful here.

to pause and reflect

ASSIGNMENT:

This week, practice actually "talking to" God. Each night before retiring, take out a pad of paper and a pen and write down a question about your life on which you would like God's guidance or input.

In the morning, just after awakening and before you do anything else, reach for the pen and paper and write down the first thing which comes to you after re-reading the question.

Do not try to "think" this answer. Simply write whatever comes to you. As soon as you start "thinking" about it, put the pen down. The first few times you do this you may only get a word or a phrase before your mind begins "getting in the way." As you continue with this practice you may find that larger gulps of information – entire phrases and whole sentences – are coming to you.

Now check these thoughts against the yardstick you were given in CWG on pages 4 and 5. Write a brief report for delivery to your group next week, or make an entry in your journal, about what you observed.

Additional Inquiries
from Chapter 2

1. What gender is God?
2. What things generate God's disapproval?
3. What can human beings create which is outside of God's plan?
4. What is evil?
5. If there were such a thing as "sin," what would it be?
6. How badly does God want our worship and obedience?
7. What is the beginning of all creation?
8. What are the Five Attitudes of God?
9. What should we all do with our presently held personal values?
10. Matthew, Mark, Luke, and John walked with Jesus and wrote his story. *True or False?*

Chapter 3
The Holy Triad

In order to understand our true nature as creative beings, it is necessary to comprehend the nature of God – the greatest creator of all – and then to really accept that we have been made *in God's image and likeness.*

Conversations with God says that God is a Triune Being.

TEXT REFERENCE:

I am manifested as Three-In-One. Some of your theologians have called this Father, Son and Holy Spirit. – *page 73*

Some of the world's religions balk at this three-level aspect of God, mainly because they hold that there is only one God. Yet it may be that this presents only a semantic difference. The fact is, God *is* One Being, and there is only One God. Yet this One God tells us It is divided into three parts, consisting of three distinct energies, and can be made manifest in many forms. . .including what we would call higher and lower aspects of Itself. This leads us to the next concept in *CWG*. For if human beings are made in the "image and likeness of God," then it stands to reason that. . .

CONCEPT #11
Human beings consist of three distinct energies.

These energies are our creative tools. They are the divine devices with which God has made it possible for us to fashion the fabric of our experience. This has already been discussed in Concept #3.

(You will note that *CWG* often circles back into itself. That is, the text of the book is circular, returning to many of the same points over and over again, revisiting the same wisdoms in different forms.)

We are literally creating ourselves with these devices, and recreating ourselves anew in every moment of Now using these tools:

1. Thought
2. Word
3. Deed

Individually, as well as collectively, these creative energies have the power to produce our reality, which we might call an *experience.*

Once we understand this, we are far more able to understand both how we got to where we are today, as well as how to get to where we wish to be tomorrow. Until we understand this, we might imagine ourselves (and all others) to be victims of situations and circumstances beyond individual control. It could certainly look that way in daily life, which is why it is difficult for most people to believe in their own creative power.

Yet nothing exists in the world which did not first exist as pure thought.

If you have not experienced what you want in your life, it is not because God has failed to answer your prayers. Rather, it is because you have been thinking, speaking, or acting in contradiction to what you have been desiring.

Throughout your life, you are operating within the framework of an immutable law. This law states that how you think, speak, or act will be reflected in your reality. It *must* be. *This is the law of the universe.*

It does no good to think one thing and do another. Or to say one thing and think another. When you do this you are at cross purposes with yourself, and your results (experiences) will be very much a "mixed bag." It will be difficult to achieve any kind of consistency in your life and in what you are creating for yourself.

Most people's lives are inconsistent for this very reason. They can't seem to "get it all together." That is, they don't seem to be able to create consistency between what they think, say, and do often enough.

EXERCISE

Let's see how much consistency there is between what you think, say and do. Following each of the words below, complete the statements which describe your thoughts, words or deeds regarding them more often than not.

MONEY:

Most often what I think about money is

____

Most often what I say about money is

____

Most often what I do about money is

____

SEX:

Most often what I think about sex is

____

Most often what I say about sex is

____

Most often what I do about sex is

____

GOD:

Most often what I think about God is

____

Most often what I say about God is

____

Most often what I do about God is

____

LOVE:

Most often what I think about love is

____

Most often what I say about love is

____

Most often what I do about love is

____

TITHING (Giving 10% to church or charity):
Most often what I think about tithing is

Most often what I say about tithing is

Most often what I do about tithing is

ONENESS:
Most often what I think about oneness is

Most often what I say about oneness is

Most often what I do about oneness is

MY LIFE'S WORK:
Most often what I think about my life's work is

Most often what I say about my life's work is

Most often what I do about my life's work is

WORLD HUNGER:
Most often what I think about world hunger is

Most often what I say about world hunger is

Most often what I do about world hunger is

MY FAMILY (Spouse, children, or loved ones):
Most often what I think about my family is

___

Most often what I say about my family is

___

Most often what I do about my family is

___

MY HEALTH:
Most often what I think about my health is

___

Most often what I say about my health is

___

Most often what I do about my health is

___

MY BODY:
Most often what I think about my body is

___

Most often what I say about my body is

___

Most often what I do about my body is

___

MY FUTURE:
Most often what I think about my future is

___

Most often what I say about my future is

___

Most often what I do about my future is

___

You may wish to continue this exercise by creating your own list of additional words which carry meaning for you, and completing the same statements about them. After you are done, open the process to discussion in your group.

to pause and reflect

ASSIGNMENT:

This week at home, answer the following questions about the above exercise in your personal journal, and come prepared to discuss them at the next class.

1. *What did you discover after doing the above exercise?*
2. *If there were any areas of inconsistency, what where they?*
3. *What did this reveal to you about yourself?*
4. *What commitment are you now willing to make to alter the inconsistency between what you think, say and do on these subjects?*
5. *When are you willing to begin?*
6. *How do you think your life would change if you did that?*

Chapter 3, Section 2
Hey, what's the big idea?

Chapter 3 of *Conversations with God* opens with a series of questions, the first of which is, *"When will my life finally take off? What does it take to 'get it together,' and achieve even a modicum of success? Can the struggle ever end?"*

The answer to these questions may very well be contained in the answers you gave to the six questions you were asked to answer in the last assignment. Those six questions revolve around your use of the three distinct energies which comprise your being.

It is important to understand that what you do with these energies, how you work with them, has everything to do with what is created in your life. (Not a little to do with it. *Everything* to do with it.)

CONCEPT #12
All you see in your world is the outcome of your idea about it.

The above statement is found on page 75 of *CWG*. It could be the most important statement in the book. If the statement is true, then it becomes extremely advantageous for us to go immediately to our highest thought about everything, and everyone, important to us.

Some people have not been in touch with their "highest thoughts" (much less their highest words or actions) for a long time. Cynicism, defensiveness, and fear have kept them from it. How about you?

EXERCISE

The exercise on pages 80-82 of this Guidebook asked you to describe your usual thoughts, words, and actions surrounding certain subjects. That list of subjects is reproduced on the next page. Now, reviewing what you wrote, make an assessment of the statements you made about each subject.

Place a check in the column where the statements you made about the various subjects represent your highest thought, word, or deed with regard to them.

YOUR HIGHEST:	THOUGHT	WORD	DEED
Money			
Sex			
God			
Love			
Tithing			
Oneness			
My Life's Work			
World Hunger			
My Family			
My Health			
My Body			
My Future			

In the above process it was possible to place 36 check marks on the page, 12 in each column. How many checks were you able to make? What percentage of your thoughts are your highest thoughts? What about your words? And your actions?

If you are like most people, this process may have shown you that, as *Conversations with God* says on page 77, "you've spent half your life unconscious. That is to say, unaware on a conscious level *of what you are choosing* in the way of thoughts, words, and deeds until you experience the aftermath of them. Then, when you experience these results, you deny that your thoughts, words, and deeds had anything to do with them."

Further discussion: ***Are you up to what you're "up to"?***

All of life is a process of creation. We are now going to enter into a creative process as part of this Guidebook.

Even if, in some instances, your thought, word, or deed with regard to the subjects above *was* your very highest, it is still possible now to create something even higher. For the true Master knows that when the highest state is reached, the "game" is over. . .unless an even higher state is imagined.

It is our "job," therefore, to continue imagining higher, and even higher, states of being – higher thoughts, word and deeds – in order that we might continue creating ourselves anew in the next grandest version of the greatest vision ever we had about ourselves.

This is, to put it in one sentence, what we are all "up to" here. It is what *God* is up to. This is God "Godding!"

So, one more time. . .here is our list of subjects. In the space provided, create now your highest idea of what you can think, say, and do about each of these topics as they relate to your life.

MONEY:

The highest thing I can think

___

The highest thing I can say

___

The highest thing I can do

___

SEX:

The highest thing I can think

___

The highest thing I can say

___

The highest thing I can do

___

GOD:

The highest thing I can think

___

The highest thing I can say

___

The highest thing I can do

___

LOVE:

The highest thing I can think

___

The highest thing I can say

___

The highest thing I can do

___

TITHING (Giving 10% to church or charity):
The highest thing I can think

The highest thing I can say

The highest thing I can do

ONENESS:
The highest thing I can think

The highest thing I can say

The highest thing I can do

MY LIFE'S WORK:
The highest thing I can think

The highest thing I can say

The highest thing I can do

WORLD HUNGER:
The highest thing I can think

The highest thing I can say

The highest thing I can do

MY FAMILY (Spouse, children, or loved ones):
The highest thing I can think

The highest thing I can say

The highest thing I can do

MY HEALTH:
The highest thing I can think

The highest thing I can say

The highest thing I can do

MY BODY:
The highest thing I can think

___

The highest thing I can say

___

The highest thing I can do

___

MY FUTURE:
The highest thing I can think

___

The highest thing I can say

___

The highest thing I can do

___

to pause and reflect

EXPERIMENT

Throughout the next week, see if you can call forth your Highest Thought about some of the things going on around you. Carry a small spiral notebook with you and make a note of the occurrences of your life – and the thoughts you now choose to have about them. See if this in any way changes your words and actions – and thus, your life.

Chapter 3, Section 3

Big dividends from small change

What you did in the last Experiment is enter into the highest form of creation. You have been deliberately re-creating yourself anew, using the three tools, or energies, with which God has equipped you. The exercise in Concept #12 of this chapter suggests that it is possible to think thoughts, say words, and undertake deeds which are not reactions, but are creations. *Deliberate* creations. It is by this process that you change your life.

The recommendation of *CWG* on this subject could have been the directions for that last Exercise.

TEXT REFERENCE:

Go to your Highest Thought about yourself. Imagine the you that you would be if you lived that thought every day. Imagine what you would think, do and say, and how you would respond to what others do and say.

Do you see any difference between that projection and what you think, do and say now? — *page* 77

The next concept we will explore relates directly to Concept #12. All you see in your world *is* the outcome of your idea about it. You have created, and have *been* creating, your entire reality. So if there is presently anything in your reality you do not now choose, *choose again*.

What is important for you to understand is that you *do* have the opportunity to do so. Nothing remains the same. Nothing.

Not even God.

CONCEPT #13

All conditions are temporary. Nothing stays the same. Which way a thing changes depends on you.

Take a close look at what's being said here. Let's explore it together.

EXERCISE

Make a list of "Things Which Have Changed" in your life, and next to each change make an analysis of whether you experienced yourself as being at the effect of that change, or as being the conscious creator of it. We've begun the list for you, to give you a jump start. Add to this list things which have changed which only you could know about – things which are specific to your life.

CIRCUMSTANCES IN MY LIFE WHICH HAVE CHANGED	Check here if this change is one which you deliberately created	Check here if this change is one which you "watched happen"
MY LIFE WORK		
The 1st time this changed	☐	☐
The time after that	☐	☐
Last time	☐	☐
MY LIFE PARTNER		
The 1st time this changed	☐	☐
The time after that	☐	☐
Last time	☐	☐
MY HEALTH		
The 1st time this changed	☐	☐
The time after that	☐	☐
Last time	☐	☐
MY PLACE OF RESIDENCE		
The 1st time this changed	☐	☐
The time after that	☐	☐
Last time	☐	☐
MY INCOME		
The 1st time this changed	☐	☐
The time after that	☐	☐
Last time	☐	☐
MY CITY'S MAYOR		
The 1st time this changed	☐	☐
The time after that	☐	☐
Last time	☐	☐
MY. . .(add to this list yourself)	☐ ☐ ☐	☐ ☐ ☐

Further discussion: *The secret of improving your quality of life*

For most people the idea that change is inevitable in life is neither a new idea, nor a startling one. What may be startling, however, is the degree to which we *control* or *create* the changes in our lives.

To a very large degree it could be said that *the quality of your life will depend upon the degree to which you control or create the changes which affect it.*

The Exercise above was designed to give you an at-a-glance assessment of how you have been doing in this regard.

to pause and reflect

ASSIGNMENT:

Throughout the upcoming week keep a record of everything that changes in your life. Appointments, dates, conditions. . .it doesn't matter. Just keep track of what is changing.

Then, next to each change you have noted, make an entry which denotes whether you were active in creating that change, or found yourself merely at the effect of it.

At the end of the week calculate what percentage of the time you were in each category. Bring this information to your class next week, or write it in your journal.

Chapter 3, Section 4
Change your purpose in life

Some people may choose now to change their purpose in life, realizing that the purpose of their life is to change (that is, to evolve).

Let me say that again, because it may be a new idea to you. I said that the *purpose of life is to change.* Perhaps you have never thought of it this way. Nevertheless, this is the way it is.

Now to some people this is the most exciting statement ever made. To others, it is the most depressing, because they have spent their whole lives trying to stay the same, to achieve *stability.* They have been seeking *changelessness* in a universe which knows nothing about such a condition, and therefore cannot produce it.

As I pointed out earlier, even God never stops changing. And to many, this could be the most depressing truth of all. For many of those who point to an ever-changing world as evidence of the chaos (and evil) in life often point to a Never-Changing God as their port in the storm; their refuge and their strength. The idea that God, too, is ever changing is to these people more than a discouraging thought. It is a blasphemy. Their deepest beliefs are rooted in the thought that God is the Great UNchanged.

Yet *Conversations with God* tells us that not only is God ever-changing, but this constant change is the *point of all life.* Or, to put this another way. . .

> *If you saw every life event as a process of evolution, would it change the way you viewed those events in your life and the lives of others?*

CONCEPT #14
The purpose of the Soul is evolution.

Change, of course, can produce what some people call "bad things." Yet change – evolution – is inevitable. This may help to explain why "bad things happen to good people," as some put it.

Without a doubt the most difficult aspect of this concept of ourselves as the creator of our own reality is the trouble many people have understanding why we, why *anyone,* would bring so-called negative experiences into creation.

A question I am asked with understandable frequency has to do, for instance, with the little children of the world. "Why would an innocent little child call upon itself physical torture and abuse, sexual molestation, and other terrible experiences such as kidnapping, and even death? Surely you cannot be saying these children are creating that for themselves!"

We can only grasp this fine point of metaphysics through a deeper understanding of Concept 14.

TEXT REFERENCE:

The soul is very clear that its purpose is evolution. . .it is not concerned with the achievements of the body or the development of the mind. These are all meaningless to the soul.

The soul is also very clear that there is no great tragedy involved in leaving the body. In many ways the tragedy is being *in* the body. So you have to understand, the soul sees this whole death thing differently. – *page 82*

Our comprehension is further enhanced when we begin to see how the Law of Opposites plays its effect in our lives, assisting us in creating, being, and experiencing Who We Really Are.

This law, explained in detail in several sections of *CWG* and discussed in Chapter 1, Section 5 of this Guidebook, holds that in the Realm of the Relative, which we have co-created and in which we reside, nothing can be anything without its exact opposite. (See Concept #5, page 53.)

Many people live an entire lifetime and fail to embrace this extraordinary wisdom. Yet *Conversations with God* confronts us with it again and again, circling back around to it even as we have done here, urging us to delve into its truth, experience its mystery-solving clarity, and thus step into gratefulness for every life experience. For the Soul must ultimately experience "all of it" in order to experience itself as *any* of it.

TEXT REFERENCE:

How can it be up if it has never been down, left if it has never been right? How can it be warm if it knows not cold, good if it denies evil? Obviously, the Soul cannot choose to be anything *if there is nothing to choose from.* – *Page 84*

EXERCISE

Make a list of the last three major decisions you made about your life, or the last three things you decided about yourself (I am good, I am abundant, I am loved, etc.). Now, going back in your memory, think of the first few experiences which life brought you in the immediate aftermath of your decision.

A CHOICE I RECENTLY MADE	THE FIRST THING I CAN REMEMBER WHICH HAPPENED AFTER THAT
1.	
2.	
3.	

to pause and reflect

ASSIGNMENT:

This week, look to see how the Law of Opposites plays its effect in your life by continuing the above exercise all week. List the important choices you make this week, then fill out column 2. See if you can begin to identify any apparently opposing forces as friendly energies, bringing you golden opportunities to decide and declare, become and express, experience and fulfill your next grandest idea of Who You Really Are.

Chapter 3, Section 5
Who do you think you are, anyway?

When I was a small boy I was the kind of youngster some people would call a "smart alec," and my father had occasion to ask me innumerable times, "Who do you think you *are,* anyway?" I've spent the rest of my life trying to answer that question.

You are trying to answer that question, too – whether you know it or not. That is really the only question in life. Who do you think you are, anyway? Of this I can assure you: who you *think* you are is exactly who you will wind up being.

CONCEPT #15
You are who you think you are. You are your own thoughts about yourself, made manifest.

Now there may be somewhat of a "gap" between who you think you are and Who You Really Are.

(Whenever those last four words appear in the book *Conversations with God,* you will notice they are always capitalized. That is because Who You Really Are is a Being of such magnitude, any reference to that deserves to be capitalized.)

This gap is the difference between your thought about you and God's thought about you. If you thought about you the way God thinks about you, you'd smile a lot. But most people do not think of themselves the way God thinks of them; they do not see themselves the way God sees them, and they do not conceive of themselves as being the way God *knows* them to be.

It is as God Herself put it in *CWG:* "If I told you that you are born of God – that you are pure Gods and Goddesses at birth – pure love – you would reject me. All of your life you have spent convincing yourself that you are bad. Not only that you are bad, but that the things you want are bad. Sex is bad, money is bad, joy is bad, power is bad, having a lot is bad – *a lot of anything*. . .No, no, my friend, you may not be very clear about many things, but about one thing you are clear: you, and most of what you desire, are bad."

Because so many people hold these thoughts, I thought it important to devote one very small section of this Guidebook to one very large message. This is that section. You will note that it has no exercises, no assignments, and no experiments to suggest. Just a little wisdom from *CWG* itself about Who You Really Are.

If you are confused about this, why not take a look at how God sees you?

TEXT REFERENCE:

You are goodness and mercy and compassion and understanding. You are peace and joy and light. You are forgiveness and patience, strength and courage, a helper in time of need, a comforter in time of sorrow, a healer in time of injury, a teacher in times of confusion.

You are the deepest wisdom and the highest truth; the greatest peace and the grandest love. You *are* these things, and in moments of your life you have *known* yourself as these things. *Choose now to know yourself as these things always.*

— Page 87

to pause and reflect

Additional Inquiries
from Chapter 3

1. We have made a covenant with God regarding the creation process. What is our role in this covenant?
2. The creation process involves aligning three aspects of ourselves to produce a result or experience. What are these three aspects?
3. What is the Divine purpose behind our forgetting Who We Really Are?
4. What does God get out of this process of our re-creating Who We Really Are?

5. What are the first steps to having your life "take off"?
6. Name some of the ways *CWG* says your life would improve if you followed these steps.
7. How do you call forth (re-create) yourself?
8. The best way to handle a painful experience in life is to. . .
9. What is the soul's desire?
10. The soul seeks only good feelings. *True or false?*
11. What is result of our thinking of ourself as "bad"?
12. It is prideful and nonbeneficial to the soul to think of ourselves as good or Godly. *True or False?*

Chapter 4
Stop Trying to Learn

Not long ago I was pulled aside by a young woman attending one of my lectures. "How can I learn more about myself?" she asked me with great earnestness, then explained, "I am on a journey of self-discovery."

"No, you're not," I replied. "Your life has nothing to do with self-discovery. And you have nothing to learn."

"I don't?" she echoed, a bit taken aback.

"No, you don't," I assured her. Then I told her to stop looking all over the place for "the answers" – whatever *they* are – and start looking for the *questions* – the inquiries which are most important in her life – and *give them answers.*

(I am reminded here of a story I heard about Gertrude Stein on her death bed. The room was filled with family and friends as she looked up in one of her final moments and cried plaintively, "What is the *answer?*"

Silence hung heavy.

"In that case," said Gertrude Stein, "what is the question?")

CONCEPT #16
Life is not a process of discovery; it is a process of creation.

Our lives seem dotted with questions from beginning to end. And for most of us life has become a process of seeking to discover the answers. We say that we are trying to "find ourselves," that we are "truth seekers," and so forth. Yet in this, sincere as we may have been, we may have had it all backward.

TEXT REFERENCE:
You do not live each day to *discover* what it holds for you, but to *create* it. You are creating your reality every minute, probably without knowing it. – *Page 91*

When we decide to *provide* answers rather than seek them, we have graduated from Beginning Student to Intermediate. The next step is Advanced Student. Then. . .Master.

Of course, I have made these rankings up. I use them simply to make a point. The place God would have us occupy in our universe is the place called Creator. Anything less than that is a lie about us.

EXERCISE

Turn to page 91 in *CWG* and review the Ten Point Path to Realization of Self as Creator. Take turns reading these aloud in your study group, or, if you are studying alone, read them into a tape recorder and play them back so that you may hear them read to you.

NOTE: You may wish to play this tape back every day. For study groups: you may find it beneficial and inspirational to read these ten points aloud before some of your meetings as a part of your opening ritual.

Further discussion: *Hold fast to your original creative thought.*

Committing these ten steps to memory will allow you to "wake up." You will no longer be sleepwalking through your life, but will be consciously aware of what you are thinking, saying, and doing – and of the impact that is having in your life.

You will then have a chance to change anything you are thinking, saying, or doing which is not in harmony with what you choose to call forth in your life. *CWG* invites you to "throw all negative thoughts out of your mental constructions. Lose all pessimism. Release all doubts. Reject all fears. Discipline your mind to hold fast to your original creative thought."

You can train yourself to do this. "Look," says *CWG,* "how well you have trained yourself not to do it."

to pause and reflect

EXPERIMENT

Using the same notebook you used in your last experiment, begin a diary of any questions about life (they can be "important" or "not important," it doesn't matter) which come to you as you walk through your days this week. Call this your Creation Diary. At the end of each day review this list of questions, and give each of them an answer. If you don't know the answer (careful, here comes the powerful part), *make one up*. Give the question the answer which best suits you.

Write out your answers. (Putting them in writing gives them strength, power.) Make a commitment to turn these ideas into reality with every new thought, word, and deed which issues forth from you, beginning the very next day.

EXPERIMENT - PART II

As the second part of this week's experiment, try moving through the next seven days *without asking anyone else any questions at all.* See if it is possible for you to move through your life without ever asking anyone a question again.

This could be a spectacular affirmation of the Truth that you have within you enormous knowledge, understanding, and power, as well as the ability to call forth from sources outside of yourself whatever data and information you need to activate your inner resources and create whatever you choose.

HERE'S A TIP. You can cause the universe to bring you any information you need by simply turning questions into "commands."

Example:

"What time is it?"
becomes
"Please tell me what time it is."

"Do you know the way to San Jose?"
becomes
"I wish to know the way to San Jose, please."

You will discover (perhaps much to your astonishment) that the world will jump to give you what you call forth in this way. (Especially when you do so quietly and nicely.)

Next week, come to the study group ready to share your experience. What did it bring up for you? If you are studying *CWG* alone, make an entry about this in your journal.

Additional Inquiries
from Chapter 4

1. What is the one way we can take the wrong path and not reach our goal of returning to God?
2. Why is man's continuing attempt to "find himself" and to discover the secret of life doomed to failure?
3. (Review question) What are the three aspects of our being involved in creation?
4. What is the relationship between knowing and gratitude?
5. Why is it undesireable to condemn events or actions you don't like?
6. Why do we so often create events which are not what we want?
7. What is the best way to avoid creating what you don't want?

Chapter 5

How God Takes Command

God is "in command" of the entire universe, and all of life. Of this there is no question. On this every religion in the world agrees. (It is probably the only thing on which every religion in the world agrees!) The real question is, how does God "take command"? How does She exercise Her Absolute Power? How does He demonstrate His Supreme Authority? On this, many of the world's religions *disagree*.

CWG provides us with a startling new answer to these questions. God, the manscript says, *does not take command at all*. That is, God is "in command" without commanding.

TEXT REFERENCE:

Who would I command? Myself? And why would such commandments be required? Whatever I want, is, *n'est ce pas*? How is it therefore necessary to command anyone?

— Page 95

To this answer God adds God's own stunning question: "How could I wish something to be so *so badly that I would command it*, and then sit by and watch it not be so? What kind of a king would do that? What kind of a ruler?"

The answer is none, of course. God declares that He is neither a king nor a ruler, but simply, and awesomely, the Creator. And, as the Creator, God performs one function, and one function only. She creates, creates, and keeps on creating. That is, presumably, spectacular enough. God does not need to rule over His creations with an iron hand in order for Her to get some satisfaction out of it.

All of which leads us to. . .

CONCEPT #17
There is no such thing as the Ten Commandments.

This is perhaps one of the most striking concepts in a book full of striking concepts. It is a remarkable revelation which allows the human race to at last remove itself from the place of fear with regard to God.

EXERCISE

In a round table discussion in your study group, or in your journal, answer the following questions.

1. Is it possible that this astonishing statement is true?

2. If there are no Commandments, what *did* Moses take to his people? Why and how did these become interpreted as commands from God?

3. How can the world live without the Commandments? What would stop us from doing "bad things" if there were no injunctions against them?

4. If God is the All-In-All, the Sum of Everything, the Alpha and the Omega, who would God be punishing if the Commandments were not kept?

The central issue in our relationship with God is this: Just what kind of relationship *is* it?

Is God our Lord and Master, whom we must obey under penalty worse than death? Or is God a different kind of Master, who wants and needs nothing from us, loves us without condition, and whose greatest joy is allowing us to create – *anything we wish?*

Is it possible that God really has no preference in the matter? Many people believe that God does have a personal preference regarding the way we live our lives, the choices we make, and the paths we walk. What do you think?

Let's play a little game. Let's imagine that God does have preferences, and now let's further imagine that *we know what they are.* (This is the position taken by most of the world's organized religions, of course.)

EXERCISE

Below is a list of common human experiences and activities. In the columns to the right, list your own personal preferences with regard to these experiences or activities, and then, what you imagine God's preference to be.

THE EXPERIENCE	My personal preference with regard to this	God's preference with regard to this
You are invited to enjoy an unexpected romantic sexual experience with a single person to whom you are very attracted.		
You help someone to "find God," and they are so grateful that you are offered $1,500 as their personal gift of appreciation.		
You and your lover have created a pregnancy together. Neither of you wants a child right now.		
You open up a magazine and find that it contains some very racy pictures of people with no clothes on engaging in sexual acts.		
You are offered a chance to have a couple of drinks at a party with some friends.		
You are offered a chance to have a couple of puffs of marijuana at a party with some friends.		
You are offered "big money" to write an article about the problems of the poor.		

to pause and reflect

ASSIGNMENT:

This week, keep a record of the judgments you make. Create a small Judgment Journal in a notebook and make an entry each night, allowing yourself to remember all of the judgments you made that day about any other person, place, or thing. Then make a list of the judgments you made about yourself, or something that you were being, doing, or having. Be honest. And whatever you do, don't start ***judging*** *yourself for* ***making judgments****. Just notice when you do, and enter that in your journal.*

Bring your Judgment Journal to class next week and have a group discussion about this. Make a list in class of any judgments you all have in common. Then talk about what you feel God's judgments are about these things.

Chapter 5, Section 2

The renunciation of renunciation

There have been many ideas floating around the past umteen thousand years about the Path to God, the Road to Enlightenment, the Way to Nirvana, and the holy life of truly holy men. One of the most prevalent of these ideas is that renunciation is The Way.

Actually, it is not.

At least, not necessarily.

Of course, *any* way you take is the way *to* take if it gets you where you wish to go. But one of the major messages of *CWG* is that there is no "right way" to go; no "right path" or "wrong path," but only the path which you're on.

This means that the practice of renunciation as most people understand it (in which we renounce or "give up" all earthly passions and physical indulgences), is not the only way to enlightment, nor is it even necessary in order to achieve enlightenment. It is simply one way; *a* way. It is simply one person's preference; one group's choice. Just as the Catholic Church is one person's preference; one group's choice. Just as the Baptist Church is the same. And the Jewish faith and teachings. And the Buddhist philosophy. And the Tao.

And so on and so forth, so on and so forth, so on and so forth. . .seemingly forever.

Our choices are unrestricted, our opportunities are unlimited, our paths are unending.

This may come as news to many who feel that renunciation is the only effective way to achieve mastery.

TEXT REFERENCE:

. . .self denial is not required. A true Master does not "give up" something. A true Master simply sets it aside, as he would do with anything for which he no longer has any use.

— Page 100

There is a huge difference, of course, between stepping away from something, or "setting it aside," and giving it up. There is an enormous shift in consciousness which takes place when we move from resisting something (our most passionate urges and desires) to accepting that something is there – and then simply not choosing it. Resisting our impulses and deepest urges never works for very long, for it is a great truth that. . .

CONCEPT #18
What you resist persists.

In fact, the irony of life is that the very act of resisting something *places it there.* This is so because you cannot resist something which does not exist. Therefore, your very resistence to something is an announcement to the universe that *you believe it is there.* And, of course, what you believe is what will be made manifest in your reality.

EXERCISE

Can you think of anything in your life so far which began in your experience as a "negative" thing, only to have the negativity which was attached to it drop away as soon as you dropped your resistance to it?

See if you can make a list of such things below and, if you are in a study group, share it with the others. I've named a few of my own here, just to help you get started.

Initially negative experiences which seemed not so negative at all as soon as I stopped resisting them:

SPINACH
GOING TO THE DENTIST
PAYING BILLS
LISTENING TO MY FATHER'S REPEATED "WAR STORIES"
WALKING ON THE BEACH IN OPEN-TOED CLOGS OR "FLIP-FLOPS"
HAVING MY BLOOD DRAWN
SLEEPING WITH SOMEONE WHO SNORES
READING A MASSIVE, I MEAN A REALLY MASSIVE, BOOK
SHOPPING WITH SOMEONE WHO DOESN'T KNOW WHAT THEY WANT

WAITING, ESPECIALLY IN LINES WHICH SEEM TO STALL AS SOON AS I GET IN THEM

Your list, continued. . .

____

____

____

____

____

____

____

In my life I have learned to turn these formerly negative experiences into positive ones, simply by changing my point of view about them. I have stopped resisting, and, like magic, the negativity stopped persisting. The exterior condition itself may not have changed, but *my experience of it did.*

Not only have I stopped resisting so-called negative experiences, I have also stopped resisting my passions by calling them "bad." I have stopped judging myself for having them, stopped making myself wrong. If my passion for a thing comes into play in my life, I simply notice what I have a passion for, then look to see if it serves me to indulge that passion right now – or ever.

TEXT REFERENCE:

Remember, you are constantly in the act of creating yourself. You are in every moment deciding who and what you are. You decide this largely through the choices you make regarding who and what you feel passionate about. – *Page 100*

Some passions are what you would label "good," depending upon what it is you are trying to do or be. A person may be said to have a "passion for God," for instance, or a passion to help others. Passions themselves, therefore, are not to be avoided. Indeed, it is passion which drives the engine of the human experience.

EXERCISE

List ten things for which you have had an enormous passion in your life. Dig into your past, not just your present moment, to remember some of these passions. Now, on the form below, indicate which passions serve you (help you to achieve a goal; bring you joy, goodness, benefit) today, and which do not.

Passions I have, or have had, in my life	Served me then (check here)	Serves me now (check here)	Will probably serve me in the future (check here)

Further discussion: *What does "mastery" require?*

Earlier in this section I used the phrase "renunciation as most people understand it." That choice of words was deliberate and meaningful.

What were you told you had to renounce in order to be spiritually evolved?

Most people understand renunciation as "renouncing" something. That is, condemning something, or at the very least, "giving it up," because it is "bad," "not okay," or "unhealthy" spiritually or physically. Yet the true Master understands the lighter nuance of the word as it is applied to spiritual process. To the Master, there is never any "renouncing" of anything in the sense of giving it up, and there certainly is never any condemning of anything – for the Master condemns nothing. (*"Judge not, and neither condemn. . ."*)

As *CWG* points out, to condemn a thing is to condemn God, for nothing which has been created has been created in God's absence. Thus, in condemning the creation you condemn the creator.

So the Master does not condemn, nor does the Master have the experience of "giving up" a thing. To the Master, the act of renunciation is a setting aside of something, as one sets aside the toys of one's youth when one becomes an adult. It is a stepping away from something, as one avoids a moving train, or a construction site, or a manhole. One doesn't "give up" the manhole in any sense. One simply and merely steps around it.

to pause and reflect

ASSIGNMENT:

This week, make a list of all you have stepped away from in your life so far; all that you have set aside. This may be persons, places, or things. Everything from the toys of your youth to the friendships which no longer serve you to the habits you have broken.

Do not list things that have been taken from you, but rather, only those things you have consciously set aside, stepped away from.

Then, after making this list, write in a column next to each item the reason you set this item or experience aside, and how it has served you to do so.

Finally, make a second list before next week of all that you now see no longer serves you in your life – no longer is a declaration of Who You Are – and bring that list to your study group (or write it in your journal), together with your proclamation of when you intend to step away from that or set it aside.

Chapter 5, Section 3
Expecting no more expectations

To the "renunciate," passion is everything. This is often a surprising revelation to those who would study to become Masters. Yet to the Master it is obvious.

TEXT REFERENCE:
Passion is the love of turning being into action. It fuels the engine of creation. It changes concepts to experience. . . .Never deny passion, for that is to deny Who You Are, and Who You Truly Want to Be. The renunciate never denies passion — the renunciate simply denies attachment to results. – *Page 101*

To live your life without expectation – without the need for specific results – *that* is freedom. That is Godliness.

CONCEPT #19
Passion is not expectation, and expectation is not passion.

To "have a passion" for something does not mean one necessarily has to have an expectation about it. "Having a passion" for something is what drives us to an experience. It is what motivates us, inspires us. "Having an expectation," on the other hand, generally ruins whatever we may had had a passion for.

(In the human sexual experience this is particularly, and perhaps most obviously, true – which should tell us something about expectation and passion *in all of life.*)

EXERCISE

If expectation of a particular result were removed from the equation, what reason would you have to be, do or have anything?

In the boxes below, list the last five things you can remember consciously choosing to be, do or have. Then answer the questions asked in columns A and B.

Three things I've recently chosen to BE	What I expected might happen as a result of my being this	A reason I could create to be this if there *was* no particular result
1.		
2.		
3.		

Three things I've recently chosen to DO	What I expected might happen as a result of my doing this	A reason I could create to do this if there *was* no particular result
1.		
2.		
3.		

Three things I've recently chosen to HAVE	What I expected might happen as a result of my having this	A reason I could create to have this if there *was* no particular result
1.		
2.		
3.		

Further discussion: *The question that will change your life*

There is only one reason to be, do, or have anything, and that is to announce and declare Who and What you think you Are, and Who and What you Choose to Be. This point is made over and over again in *CWG* (and repeatedly in this Guidebook).

The point of life is to create Who and What You Are, and then to experience that.

You are doing that right now, whether you know it or not. Your idea about yourself is very powerful. It dictates *all* choice – every choice you have made in your life. And ever *will* make.

For instance, if you think you are afraid, you will make choices which reflect that idea about yourself. If you think you are not afraid, you will make other choices. If you think you are angry, you will make choices which reflect that idea about yourself. If you think you are not angry, you will make another choice, and so on.

Now the trick to changing some of your longest held behaviors is to change your idea about Who and What You Are in certain circumstances.

If you can't do that, there is a secondary route (something like a smaller, slower highway that still "gets you there") which you might take. Simply ask yourself what choice you might make if you did *not* think you were angry, afraid, sad, or whatever right now. Say to your inner self, "Look, I know that you are this right now. . .but, just for the sake of exploration, what choice would you make right now if you were not?"

This is a transformational question that will change your life.

to pause and reflect

EXPERIMENT

The next time you become miffed or angry about something, ask yourself what you would choose to be, do, or have if you were *not* angry.

Use this technique any time you are experiencing yourself in a way which in the past has caused you to make choices which have not served you.

Keep a diary of when you have used the If-You-Were-Not technique this week, and what happened after you used it. Come prepared to discuss this in class next session. . .or write a commentary on it in your journal.

Additional Inquiries
from Chapter 5

1. What is the one true path to God?
2. If God does not demand that we obey the Ten Commandments, what is their meaning?
3. Where is heaven and how do we get there?
4. Why don't we experience heaven here and now?
5. Following our earthly passions is a barrier to spiritual enlightment. *True or False?*
6. What is the greatest source of man's unhappiness?
7. Why should we resist not evil nor those things we don't want in our life?
8. What is the point of life?

Chapter 6
"Suffering Succotash!"

When I was a kid one of my favorite cartoon characters was a black and white cat with a bulbous nose named Sylvester who walked on two feet, talked with a lisp, and ran around exclaiming, "*Suffering succotash!*"

In the early days I never knew what the words meant, I only knew they sounded funny. Later I learned that *suffering succotash* meant nothing at all, since succotash can't suffer.

Still later, I learned that human beings are very much like succotash. No, it isn't because many of us are walking around like vegetables (although many of us are). It is because we don't have to suffer any more than vegetables do. Most of us only think we do.

Some people, in fact, actually believe that suffering is the way and the path to God. Of course, this is not true.

TEXT REFERENCE:

I am not pleased by suffering, and whoever says I am does not know Me. Suffering is an unnecessary aspect of the human experience. It is not only unnecessary, it is unwise, uncomfortable, and hazardous to your health.

— Page 105

No God in the universe who claims to be a loving, caring, wise and righteous God would ever choose suffering for anyone or anything – much less demand it. The thought, then, that someone *must* suffer in order to meet the mandate of God is not only inaccurate, it is dangerous. Dangerous because if someone believed it, that someone might cause himself *or others* to suffer needlessly.

I have italicized the words "or others" in that sentence above because this is where society gets itself into deep trouble. Many people hold a thought *for others* which they *insist must be true for those others* – such as the thought that suffering is necessary, no matter how great or how endless it is, and therefore we are not to terminate our lives, nor to assist others in terminating theirs, no matter much suffering is going on.

The idea that *God* wants this – nay, that God *demands it* – is what drives our society's continuing (but, thank goodness, lessening) opposition to physician-assisted suicide. And while I do not wish this Guidebook to become a political science text, I do think bringing up such a point here is valid in that it dramatically illustrates how we as groups and individuals create, and live by, certain beliefs out of a distorted and inaccurate view of what is true.

So perhaps it is time now to fully understand and fully accept this truth:

CONCEPT #20
Suffering is not necessary.

This may upset many apple carts (to say nothing about putting an end to many "dramas"), but it has to be said. It is another of the many important points in the book you are studying.

I am going to make a statement now which you may never have seen anywhere; may never have heard before in quite this way:

SUFFERING IS A POINT OF VIEW

I know this is difficult to believe – and even for those who believe, difficult to accept. Yet it is true. And *CWG* makes it clear this is true.

EXERCISE

Read pages 105 to 109 of *CWG* aloud (if you are in a study group, take turns reading a paragraph or two). Now complete the form below.

TIMES I HAVE SUFFERED

Make a list of five times you have suffered in your life.
(Include both physical and mental hurts.)

I SUFFERED THE TIME THAT. . .

1.____

2.____

3.____

4.____

5.____

Now answer the following questions with regard to each of these moments:

Do you think you would suffer the same way if this occurred tomorrow instead of when it did?

If yes, why do you think so?

If no, why not?

Why did you consider the above "suffering"? What would you call it if it weren't "suffering"?

What does this tell you about suffering? About yourself?

to pause and reflect

ASSIGNMENT:

Between now and the next time your study group meets (or you return to your individual work with this Guidebook), choose not to suffer.

Additional Inquiries
from Chapter Six

1. Why doesn't God just make it possible for us to put an end to suffering?
2. What is the purpose of suffering?
3. What is our largest barrier to joy?
4. What is the best way to determine if the suggestions for happiness and fulfillment provided in *CWG* are the best ways to go about finding them?

Chapter 7

The Path of the Householder

Walking the path of the Householder is not easy.

There is the story about the woman whose friend had just returned from visiting with a guru atop a mountain in some distant place. When the friend arrived home she gushed about the guru for days. Finally the woman said, "Tell me, how many children does this man have?"

"Children?" the friend could hardly believe her ears. "Why, he has no children. He's a guru. Very wise and very evolved."

"I see," the woman said. "Well, how long has he been married?"

"Married?" her friend gulped. "You don't understand. He's a *guru*. Guru's don't *get* married. That's way beneath him. He has no need for sex or romance or that kind of thing. He is very wise and very evolved."

"Ummm," the woman nodded, understanding now. "When he gets married and has children, have him call me," she said. "Until then, he don't know nothin'."

There are not many people alive today who have not dreamt at least once of having nothing more to do than sit quietly all day and enter into silent conjecture on the Nature of Being. The guru on the mountaintop, the monk in his cell, the nun in seclusion in her convent, all have been the subject of the envy of others from time to time. The contemplative life may not be for everyone, but it sure looks good to everyone every now and then.

It is not only the Contemplative, but also the Householder, who does well to dwell on Higher Things. Yet getting, and staying, in touch with grander notions and grander visions and grander understandings – and thus, your grander self – is not a thing done casually.

TEXT REFERENCE:

This is a day-to-day, hour-to-hour, moment-to-moment act of supreme consciousness. It is a choosing and a re-choosing every instant. It is ongoing creation. . .using the tools of creation we have discussed, and using them with awareness and sublime intention. – *Page 113*

Do you believe that your purpose in life is to assist and support others—your spouse, your children, your family?

Yet when one "plays the spiritual game" full out, one suddenly realizes that life's purpose is not what it was thought to be. It has nothing to do with what most of us have been spending the bulk of our time doing. It has nothing to do with putting a roof over our head, clothes on our backs, and food in our mouths. And it certainly has nothing to do with doing this for others.

And yet – and here is the irony – when we live a truly spiritual life, we find ourselves doing exactly this! That is, we find ourselves putting roofs over our head, clothes on our backs, and food in our mouths, *virtually without effort.* We also find ourselves *doing this for others* – as a *natural turn of events.*

This is because abundance and happiness follow as a natural consequence of spiritual wisdom and clarity. Put another way, once you know Who You Are, what you *have* multiplies magnificently. Sufficient, in fact, to give it away without missing any of it.

And in giving away what you yourself had once always wanted, you empower others to notice that they, too, live in a world of abundance and non-scarcity. Soon, they discover that they, too, can be (indeed, *have been*) the source of their own abundance and happiness – and that they no longer need you. That is your greatest moment. For you have done more than just *source* them, you have *empowered* them to be their *own* source.

Thus, giving power to others very soon creates your no longer *needing* to give power to others. . .for power begets power, just as love begets love, and life begets life, in all its wonderful forms.

This is "playing the spiritual game," and what the "spiritual game" calls upon you to do, *God is doing all the time.* And that is why *CWG* says that God's greatest moment is the moment you realize. . .

CONCEPT #21
You need no God.

This is an astonishing statement – one of hundreds of astonishing statements in *CWG* – because it turns all of our previous understandings upside-down. All of our lives we have been told that we need God. Not only that we need God, but that God *needs* us to need Him, and if we even *say* that we don't (much less *act like it*), we displease God, and incur His wrath.

So we have this dysfunctional God we have imagined Who demands that we need Him *or else.*

EXERCISE

Turn to page 114 in *CWG* and begin reading the italic type three sentences from the bottom. Read until the italic type ends on the top of page 115.

This is one of the most eloquent statements of eternal truth ever written. Discuss now with your study group — or in writing in your journal if you are studying alone — what these six extraordinary statements mean to you.

Answer the following questions:

1. Do you believe, in particular, Statements 5 and 6?

2. If you do, what does that imply in your life? What does that mean to you?

Further discussion: *Did God create the problem? Is this a test?*

Most people find it difficult to fit themselves into the scenario of empowerment laid out above. They do not see themselves providing life's necessities "virtually without effort." Just the opposite. They see themselves making a great deal of effort – and in many cases getting nowhere. They feel "stuck," trapped. And far from seeing themselves as not needing God, they turn to God to ask for help in getting out of the "traps" of their life. Some even believe that God created the problem! They see it as a "test" given them by God, and beg that the test be over, that the time of trial be ended.

EXERCISE

Now it's time to play "Traps I Am In." This is an exciting game that many people are playing without knowing it. It relates directly to the idea that, as a person walking the Path of the Householder, it is virtually impossible to lead a life which includes time to contemplate (much less experience) spiritual truth. Play the game below by filling in the squares. After all the squares are filled in, hold a round table discussion with your study group. (You may want to break into smaller groups to facilitate this process so that everyone has a chance to share.)

TRAPS I AM IN

In the spaces below, make a list of some "traps" in which you now find yourself.

Maybe you feel trapped in a job you don't like, or in a relationship that is not working, or in a behavior pattern which no longer serves you, or meeting some sort of obligation which it no longer pleases you to meet.

Whatever the case, describe the "trap" in the column at left.

Then, supply the information requested in the other three columns.

A "TRAP" I AM IN:	HOW I GOT INTO THIS TRAP	WHAT STOPS ME FROM GETTING OUT OF IT	WHAT WOULD HAPPEN IF I DID ANYWAY

Does God deliberately create dramas and difficulties in our lives to see how well we've "learned our lessons"? Of course not. God does no such thing. A re-reading of *CWG* (page 117) may be beneficial in helping to understand how God interacts with us. This passage states that God does not have any particular desires with regard to us, but rather, chooses for us what we choose for ourselves.

Here again the text of *CWG* is circular. We have visited this information before. Indeed, the chapter of *CWG* we are now studying ends with the recommendation that the material in this dialogue be read again and again "until you understand every passage. Until you're familiar with every word."

to pause and reflect

ASSIGNMENT:

This week, decide to spring free of your "traps." Choose at least one and do what it takes to get out of that.

Report on how this went to your study group next week, or make a detailed entry on your experience in your journal.

Additional Inquiries
from Chapter 7

1. What is the "process of self realization"?

2. How can we be truly helpful to those who are dependent on us for material and/or emotional support?

3. A true Master has many students. False masters have very few. *True or False?*

4. If we ask God to solve a problem and it remains unsolved, it is because:
    a. there's a lesson we need to learn
    b. we haven't earned the right to have it solved
    c. we don't understand how God interacts with us
    d. we didn't pray correctly

5. What is God's role in creating our lives?

6. Life proceeds out of our:
    a. highest thought
    b. intentions for it
    c. affirmations
    d. prayers

7. What is the best way to unlearn false teachings which keep us mired in guilt and self-recrimination?

Chapter 8
Relating to Relationship

Human relationships have caused us more trouble than any other single aspect of the life experience. That is hardly surprising, since relationships form the basis of most of that experience. Still, having said that, one would think that with all this focus on relationships through the centuries of humankind's adventure we would have come to some solutions to the problems and the challenges they present, and to some greater wisdom on the matter.

It is clear we have not. At least, not most people.

Most people are still walking around as if in a daze on the issue of relationships. They don't know how to handle them, and they don't know how to get along without them. In short, they don't know how to *relate to relationships.*

We are not supposed to get along without relationships, of course. Indeed, without relationships we are nothing. We cannot be Who We Really Are.

That is because in this, the Realm of the Relative, we can only experience ourselves *in relation to something or someone else.* (See Concept #5 in this Guidebook) In the Realm of the Absolute, whence we have come, this is not true. In that realm we and God (who are One and the Same) know Ourselves completely Right Now (which is the only "time" there is). But if we want to *experience* ourselves as that which we know ourselves to Be, we must move into the Realm of the Relative.

EXERCISE

Re-read the text which appears on pages 22-28 of *CWG*. Do not skip this short review. It will be very valuable for you to re-read this material right now. Then answer the following questions in your journal, or in your study group.

1. What is the reason your soul left the Realm of the Absolute and now lives inside your body in this physical world?
2. Why does God not simply experience Himself as Who He Is in the Realm of the Absolute?
3. Why has God given each of us the power to create our own reality?

If you do not know the answers to these questions, study *CWG*, pages 22-28, again. A thorough understanding of these concepts will greatly facilitate your integration of the material on relationships in the chapter you are now studying.

Every relationship is a blessed gift – even those relationships which you believe to have brought you nothing but sadness and pain. When you deeply comprehend this you will understand that. . .

CONCEPT #22
All relationships are holy.

Yet this understanding does not always help us make our relationships work. Especially our romantic relationships. And when our romantic relationships fail, it is nearly always for the same reason: we got into them for the wrong reason.

TEXT REFERENCE:
Most people enter relationships with an eye toward what they can get out of them, rather than what they can put into them. The purpose of relationship is to decide what part of yourself you'd like to see "show up," not what part of another you can capture and hold. — *Page 122*

There is only one purpose for relationship – and for all of life – and that is to be and to declare, to become and to fulfill, to express and to experience Who You Really Are. *Every* relationship, with every person, place or thing, allows you to do that.

EXERCISE

Most people have an image of themselves, an idea of Who They Are. On a scale below, fill in the box to indicate Who You Are with regard to the amount or quantity you possess of the human qualities listed. (On the yardstick, 1 is the least and 10 is the most of each quality you see yourself being.)

I AM. . .	1	2	3	4	5	6	7	8	9	10
Honest							☐			
Loyal							☐			
Courageous							☐			
Beautiful / handsome							☐			
Intelligent							☐			
Considerate							☐			
Sexually sensational							☐			
Spiritually evolved							☐			
Open and transparent							☐			
Helpful							☐			
Insightful							☐			
Compassionate							☐			
Generous							☐			
An exciting person							☐			
Capable, resourceful							☐			

Further discussion: *The paradox of all human relationships*

This may be very difficult for you to believe, but you have no need for any particular Other in your life in order for you to fully experience Who You Are. And yet without *some* Other you are nothing.

For a fuller understanding of this, review Chapter 8 of *CWG* through page 127.

Then. . .

to pause and reflect

ASSIGNMENT:

Find time this next week to listen to the radio twice for at least one-half hour each time. Pick a station playing popular or country music. As you listen, make a log of the songs you hear. Rate each song according to the chart below.

NAME OF SONG	Song is sad	Song is happy	Song is about "one special other"	Song is about how all others are special

How many songs said that the singer "can't live without" that certain other? ______________

What does this tell you about the messages we are receiving from today's music?

____

____

____

____

How many movies have you seen which send the message summarized in the column at the far right on the previous page? Give their titles.

____

____

____

____

What does this tell you about the kinds of relationships our films model for us?

____

____

____

____

Chapter 8, Section 2

The virtue of being self-centered

If you have re-read Chapter 8 through page 127 as requested, you have already refreshed your memory on an extraordinary principle of making relationships work: self-centeredness.

It is highly beneficial in all human relationships to put yourself first.

TEXT REFERENCE:

Let each person in relationship worry not about the other, but only, only, only about *Self*. . .the most loving person is the person who is Self-centered. – *Page 124*

As *CWG* points out, this may seem a strange teaching. It violates every sense most of us have had about how relationships are supposed to function. Yet *CWG* clears up the mystery by explaining that at every moment everybody is trying to accomplish something; everybody is "up to" something every minute of every day. No action – not a single thing we do from morning 'til night – is without motivation, purpose, and reason. True, sometimes we don't *know* the reason we are doing things. Sometimes we haven't thought it all out. But at some level, your mind has already made itself up about why your body is doing "this" rather than "that," and it has instructed your body to do it.

So everything you are doing, including reading this book right now, you are doing for a *reason*. There is something you are trying to get out of it. Something you are seeking to experience. Something you hope to accomplish.

When you are clear as to what you hope to accomplish with every action you take in life, your actions themselves reflect that clarity. You become a person who is highly focused, and always "on purpose."

If you are not clear on what you are hoping to accomplish, the Principle of Self-Centeredness will make no sense to you. Or if you *are* clear, but what you have decided to accomplish is *off purpose* (that is, it has nothing to do with the reason you are on this earth, in your body, right here, right now), you will be equally mystified about the wisdom of the Principle of Self-Centeredness.

CONCEPT #23

Your purpose in life is to decide and to declare, to express and to experience Who You Really Are. This is the purpose of ALL of life.

We will keep pounding away at this until it is indelibly embedded. The *CWG* dialogue says this over and over again, in different ways. I am particularly inspired by the statement that our life purpose is to live "the grandest version of the greatest vision" we ever had about ourselves.

The grandest version of the greatest vision. That has a ring to it which for me makes everything clear. It is a standard against which I can measure everything I think, say, and do. Is this thing I am now thinking, this thing I am now saying, this thing I am now doing a reflection of the grandest version of the greatest vision I've ever had about myself?

Of course, before any of us could answer such a question, we would have to decide what that greatest vision *is*. You are going to do that now. There are many exercises in this Guidebook, but of all of those I have created, I believe this to be the most important. Please take your time with this. If you are in a study group, you may wish to devote the rest of this meeting to this exercise.

EXERCISE

Create now the "grandest version of the greatest vision" you've ever had about yourself. Use the forms below to help you.

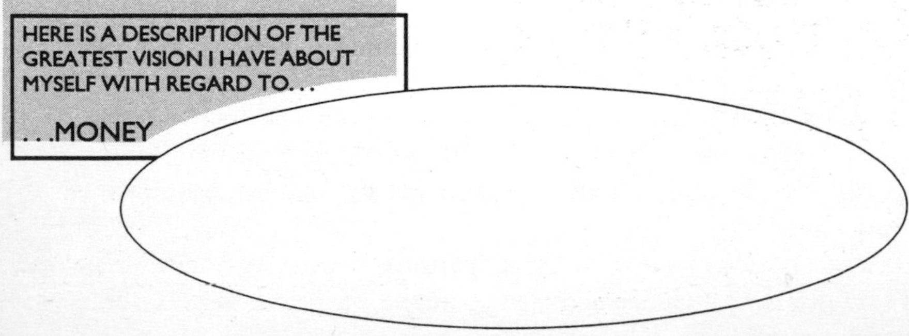

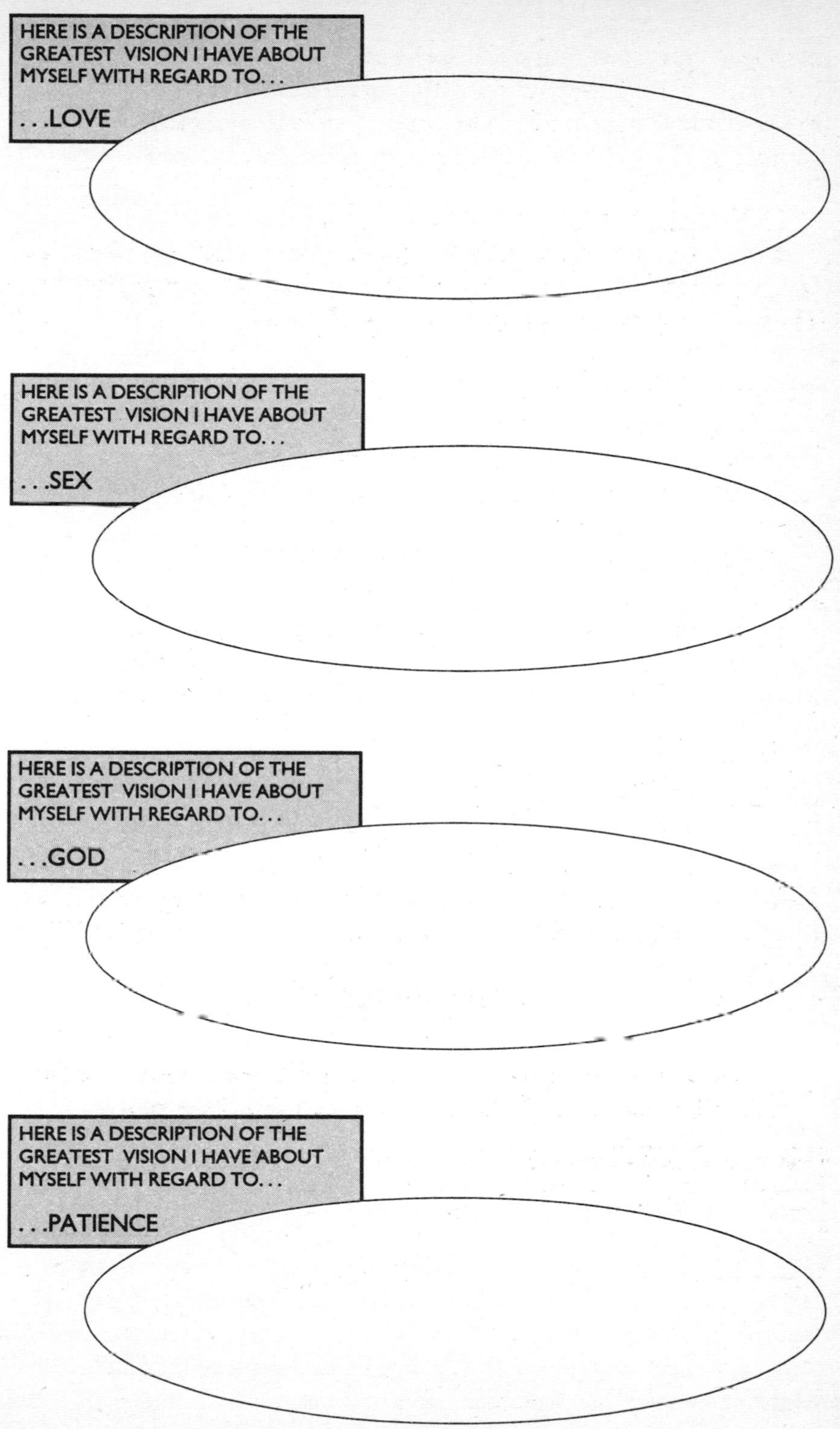
HERE IS A DESCRIPTION OF THE GREATEST VISION I HAVE ABOUT MYSELF WITH REGARD TO. . .
. . .LOVE
HERE IS A DESCRIPTION OF THE GREATEST VISION I HAVE ABOUT MYSELF WITH REGARD TO. . .
. . .SEX
HERE IS A DESCRIPTION OF THE GREATEST VISION I HAVE ABOUT MYSELF WITH REGARD TO. . .
. . .GOD
HERE IS A DESCRIPTION OF THE GREATEST VISION I HAVE ABOUT MYSELF WITH REGARD TO. . .
. . .PATIENCE

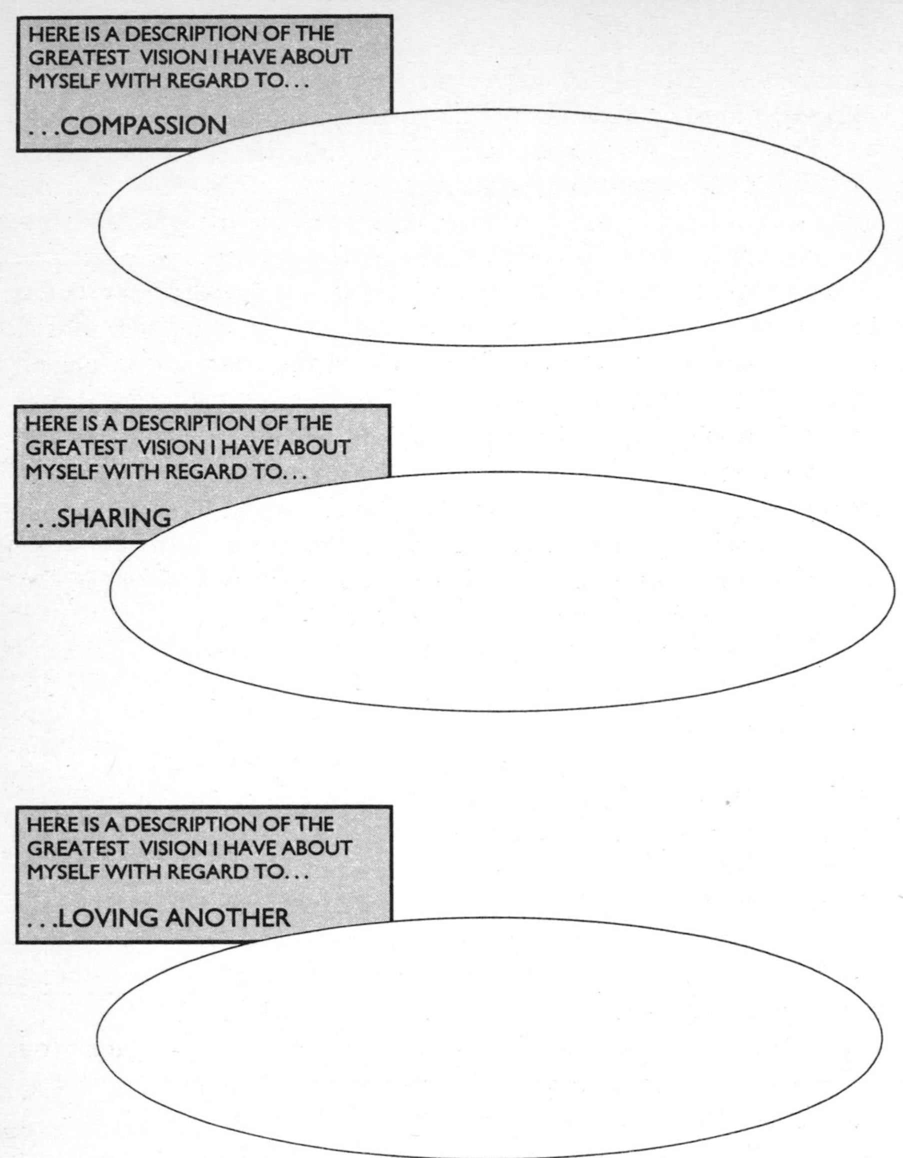

Further discussion: *The radical teaching that is not so radical*

Now perhaps it will be more clear to you that the Principle of Self-Centeredness is not so radical a teaching after all. If you still don't "get it," let me give you a very direct illustration. Suppose a person decides to devote his whole life to God and to goodness. That becomes his mission and his purpose. It becomes his highest ideal to reflect and to demonstrate goodness and Godliness. Not in order to be "good" to others, but simply (and profoundly) to bring himself the richest experience of himself he can imagine.

Now if this man has really made this decision wholeheartedly, and if he serves his purpose with every thought, word, and deed, do you think he will do any good in the world? Do you think he will touch other people's lives in a positive way? Of course he will – and he will not have done it by serving the purposes of others.

Similarily if a woman decides that Who She Is right now is the Best Mother Ever There Was, and if she makes that decision about herself joyously and wholeheartedly, and is very centered in herself with regard to this, do you think that by serving her agenda, and her agenda *only*, she will bring goodness and happiness to others? Of course she will.

You see, when your idea about yourself is *very high*, and when you do nothing all day long but *serve* that idea, you cannot *help* but be a blessing to others. In fact, we are the *highest* blessing to others when we serve the highest calling within ourselves.

> *When was the last time you explored your very reason for living, your vision about yourself, this extensively? Have you done it ever? Do you think it would help you to do it now?*

Now in the exercise above you were given an invitation to begin drawing a definition of Who You Are. You may wish to expand this exercise to include other words not on the beginning list we've provided.

Who *are* you? What is the greatest vision you have about yourself with regard to, say, war? Food stamps and public assistance to the poor? The death penalty? Abortion? Homosexuality? Gun control?

The list could go on and on – and if you are really interested in drawing a detailed portrait of yourself, it will. You will not be satisfied with just skimming the surface. You will create a list which looks at both your inner and your outer life, and defines Who You Are to the n*th* degree.

Then, if you are *truly* serious about this definition, you will go out and walk your talk. You will seek to *live* this "grandest version" of Who You Are. And you will be so joyously busy, so happily engaged in this process, that you will scarcely have time to worry about what some other person in relationship with you is up to.

You will come to know, as the Master knows, that it doesn't *matter* what your special other (or *any* other) is being, doing, having, saying, wanting, demanding. It doesn't *matter* what the other is thinking, expecting, planning. It only matters what *you* are being in *relationship* to that.

TEXT REFERENCE:

It is not in the action of another, but in your re-action, that your salvation will be found. – *Page 127*

to pause and reflect

EXPERIMENT

This week practice being self-centered. See what it feels like to do nothing which you do not want to do, given your decision about yourself regarding Who You Really Are.

While you are conducting this experiment in staying on purpose, enter into another experiment as well. Using the portrait, or definition, of yourself you have drawn here, see how many times during the upcoming week you have used your thoughts, words, and deeds to reflect that definition and to project that picture of yourself out to the world, and how many times you have not.

Carry a small spiral notebook with you and do a Morning, Noon and Night check, making entries three times a day and tabulating the number of thoughts, words, and deeds which fall into each category. That is, either they fall into Category 1 (re-presentations of your highest idea about yourself) or Category 2 (reenactments of lesser ideas about Who You Really Are).

Have fun with this. Look at it all with a smile. See the game. Enjoy the process. Don't "beat yourself up" about it if you have more Category 2's than 1's. Just look at it and see what there is to see and, if you feel it would serve you, choose differently next time.

Put your tabulations into your journal. Come to your next study group prepared to talk about what your experiments have proven.

Chapter 8, Section 3

Doing what is best for you

Throughout Chapter 8 of *CWG* the point is made over and over that you must always do what is best for you in a relationship. Always.

In Section Two of this chapter of the Guidebook it was made clear that self-centered action is by no means an action which by definition disserves another. Quite to the contrary, depending upon our idea about ourselves and our decision about how we are seeking to manifest that idea in physical form, our self-centered action may indeed produce wonderful benefit for another. Not just in thought, not just in word, but in *deed*.

The point: when you are clear what is best for you, and only *do* what is best for *you*, you never perform an unGodly act.

TEXT REFERENCE:

If, therefore, you have caught yourself in an unGodly act as a result of doing what is best for you, the confusion is not in having put yourself first, but rather in misunderstanding what is best for you. – *Page 132*

Many people refuse to do what is best for them in relationships. They've been taught that truly loving relationships require that we do what is best for our beloved Other, whether that is what is best for them or not. More often than not this leads to resentment. And sooner or later resentment ends relationships – or at the very least turns them sour. Therefore, it would be wise to contemplate. . .

CONCEPT #24
Relationships work best when you always do what is best for you.

If you keep yourself single of purpose, if you remain focused on the main chance, if you refuse to deviate from your process of recreating yourself anew in every moment of Now in the next grandest version of the greatest vision ever you had about Who You Are, you will never dis-serve another by serving yourself.

EXERCISE

Keeping in mind Who and What you have decided You Are (as described in detail through the exercise in Section Two of this chapter), let's see now how these ideas about yourself could play themselves out in everyday life. Below is a series of "life situations." Complete this exercise as if it were a game. Fill in the form and indicate what you would choose to do under the following circumstances. . .

YOU ARE TOLD by your friend Bob that he is having an affair. His wife Joanne, who is also your very good friend, later asks you about it, saying that she suspects her husband is involved with someone else, but that every time she asks him about it directly, he tells her she's hallucinating and projecting all her insecurities onto him. Joanne now is wondering whether she's crazy or what. . .she asks you for advice on how to calm her irrational fears. You listen to her beg you for guidance, and then you. . .

YOU ARE AWAKENED in the middle of the night by the sound of someone in the house. Investigating, you find a man leaving by the back door, dragging your teenage daughter through the kitchen with him. You yell for him to let your daughter go, but he does not. Your eyes light upon a cabinet drawer where you keep a gun. Lunging, you grab it, pointing it at the man and once more demanding that he release your daughter. He does not. You move toward the man and, still pointing the gun, step between him and the door. He growls, "It's her or me, bud," and threatens to strangle her if you don't let them pass. Suddenly you see an opening and you realize that with one quick trigger pull you could inflict a wound that will stop him — but will also no doubt kill him. It is clear to you in your split-second analysis that this will be your only chance. The next thing you do is. . .

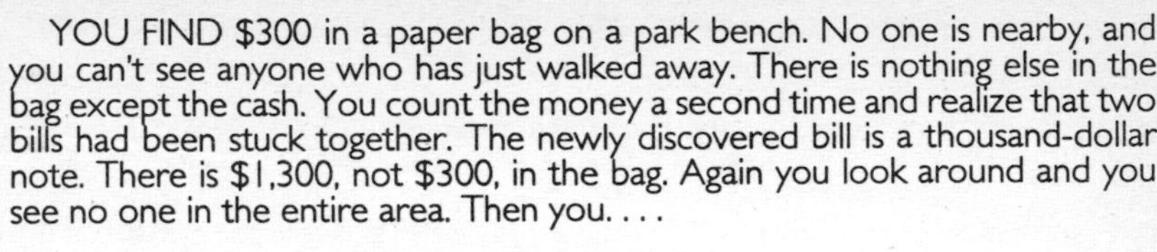

YOU FIND $300 in a paper bag on a park bench. No one is nearby, and you can't see anyone who has just walked away. There is nothing else in the bag except the cash. You count the money a second time and realize that two bills had been stuck together. The newly discovered bill is a thousand-dollar note. There is $1,300, not $300, in the bag. Again you look around and you see no one in the entire area. Then you. . . .

YOU HAVE JUST moved into a new rental home and the second day there a plain brown envelope arrives for the man who lived there before you. The property manager who rented you the house has told you that the former tenant has left the country, giving no forwarding address. You notice that there is no return address on the envelope, and just then it drops out of your hand, tearing and spilling all over the floor a series of artistic photographs of beautiful people in explicitly sexual situations. You gather the pictures up and you. . .

YOU ARE ASKED by your spouse to turn down a job you have wanted for a long time and just been offered. Your spouse makes this request because taking the job would require you and the family to move to another city, which would mean your spouse would have to leave a job that does not pay nearly as well, but that your spouse does like. You talk it over and it is clear that your spouse is not going to have a change of mind, nor see things your way and give you the green light to take the job you love and have been applying for every year for five years. Your spouse asks you to consider someone else's happiness and job satisfaction other than your own. After thinking everything over, you. . .

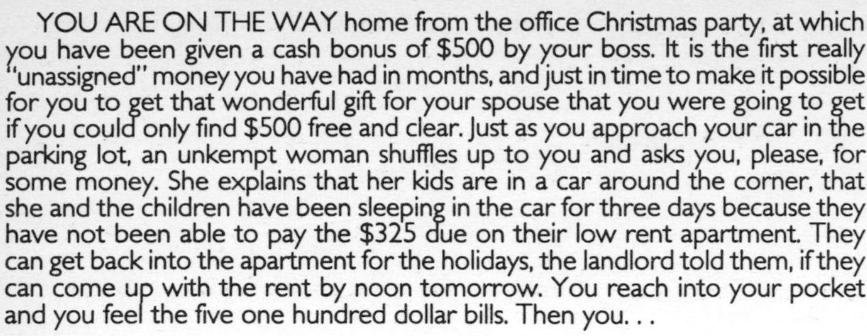

YOU ARE ON THE WAY home from the office Christmas party, at which you have been given a cash bonus of $500 by your boss. It is the first really "unassigned" money you have had in months, and just in time to make it possible for you to get that wonderful gift for your spouse that you were going to get if you could only find $500 free and clear. Just as you approach your car in the parking lot, an unkempt woman shuffles up to you and asks you, please, for some money. She explains that her kids are in a car around the corner, that she and the children have been sleeping in the car for three days because they have not been able to pay the $325 due on their low rent apartment. They can get back into the apartment for the holidays, the landlord told them, if they can come up with the rent by noon tomorrow. You reach into your pocket and you feel the five one hundred dollar bills. Then you. . .

YOU ARE IN A grocery story and you see a man slip a small package of cheese into his pocket and start out of the store. Glancing around, you see that no one but you has noticed. You then. . .

YOU ARE going into the voting booth to decide on a referendum which includes two questions on which you haven't yet made up your mind. Question A is a measure to return the death penalty to your state for crimes involving the death of another, and Question B is a measure which would bar homosexuals from filing claims of housing or job descrimination because of their sexual orientation. After reading the measures one more time in the booth, you come to your decisions about both, and you. . .

In the above "make believe" situations, did you always do what was best for you? How did you determine which course of action was "best"? You are now invited to discuss this exercise and your answers to the questions above with your group. If you are working alone, write a commentary in your journal.

Further discussion: *Looking at the obligations of relationship*

Below is a list of the obligations you have in any significant relationship. Please read the list carefully.

1.
2.
3.
4.
5.

Do you notice anything unusual about the list above? You are right. *Nothing is listed.* That's because in your relationships you have no obligations. Nor are there any restrictions, limitations, guidelines, or rules. Oh, others will try to convince you that there are, for sure. They'll even be glad to *create* some obligations, restrictions, and rules for you if you will let them. But in the eyes of God, you have none.

If this is difficult for you to accept, please read pages 135-138 in *CWG* again.

And again.

Then. . .

to pause and reflect

ASSIGNMENT:

This week move through all your relationships, business and personal, with clarity that you have no obligations in any of them. Do nothing that you feel you "have to do," and only do what you feel you choose to do, out of your decision about Who Your Are and what you choose to be, do, and have in your life.

Make a note each night about what, if anything, you did not do that you would have done before. Also make a note about all the things you continued doing exactly as you'd always done them, and explain in writing why you chose to do these things this week even though you told yourself that you didn't "have to."

Come prepared to discuss this with your study group next week.

Chapter 8, Section 4

The best wedding vows ever

We began this chapter by declaring that human relationships have caused us more trouble than any other single aspect of the life experience. We should add now, as we end it, that they've also caused us the most joy.

Yet there are no guarantees of that. Nor of anything in life. As *CWG* says, "If you want guarantees in life, then you don't want *life*. You want rehearsals for a script that's already been written."

How, then, to help ourselves get through the relationship maze with minimum trouble and maximum joy? Enter relationship with another for the *right reason*. Use your relationship for growth. Understand that it was meant for that.

Do not be deluded into thinking it is going to contain nothing but bliss (as you define it). It *will* contain nothing but bliss, which you will realize as your soul matures and you change your definition of what bliss is. For now, be willing to use it for growth; be willing to grow.

TEXT REFERENCE:

Know and understand that there will be challenges and difficult times. Don't try to avoid them. Welcome them. Gratefully. See them as grand gifts from God; glorious opportunities to do what you came into the relationship — and life — to do. – *Page 141*

And what are you seeking to grow *into?* Why, your highest *self*, of course. Remember, your purpose in life is to be Who You Really Are. You have used the exercises and the assignments in this Guidebook to once again become clear about that, and to create an even higher version of that. You have been given the chance to announce and to declare the *grandest* version of the *greatest* vision you ever had about Who You Are.

Having made this decision, having *re-created* yourself in this new and grander image, it is now only left for you to understand why it is important for you to do that. Which leads us to. . .

CONCEPT #25
You are a messenger.

Every day, every moment you send a message to the universe, to God, and to all those whose lives you touch: *This is Who I Am.*

You do it with every thought you think, every word you speak, every deed you do.

Yet not only is your message *This is Who I Am.* It is also, *This is who you can be.* With each moment of your life you are setting an example, clearing a path, showing the way.

"I am the Life and the Way," you are saying. "Follow me."

> *Is your thought about yourself large enough to see yourself as the savior of all humankind? Is it okay with you to have such a thought?*

Now most of you do not think you are saying that. In fact, most of you would never *dream* of saying that. Most of you do not want that kind of responsibility, nor do you see life as having assigned such responsibility to you.

But life has.

You have come here as a savior. You have not come here to *be* saved, but to save others. That is why it is important to work on yourself, to heal every false thought you have about yourself. (It is, no doubt, why you have been led to this Guidebook, and to the extraordinary text of *CWG* which brought you to it.) When your self-healing is over (and this can happen in an instant; it need not take forever), there will be nothing more you have to be, nothing more you have to do, nothing more you have to have in order to accept this assignment.

There will be no more workshops you have to attend, no more sermons you have to hear, no more growth groups to which you have to go. There will be no more books you have to read, no more tapes you have to listen to, no more *Guidebooks like this* you have to work through.

You may still choose to do some of these things for the sheer fun of it, for the pure enjoyment, but there will be *no more "improvements" you have to make to yourself.*

In truth, there never *were.* But you did not know that. You did not believe it. You believed instead an idea about yourself, given to you by the world, which said less about you than the truth about you.

Your false thoughts about yourself then led to actions which told a lie about you and did not show to others Who You Really Are. The Real You was not represented. That is, it was not re-*presented.* Rather than the God-in-You being presented again to all the world, you were *mis*represented. And so you have spent your time trying to make yourself "better" somehow, trying to learn all that you felt you had to learn.

You have had to learn *nothing*. You have had only to remember.

When you remember – that is, re-member. . .that is, become a member once again of the Body of God – you will see clearly that there is nothing you've ever had to learn.

You were not sent here to take care of "you." You were not sent here to somehow solve your problems. You were *given* these problems as *gifts*, divine oppportunities to choose and to declare, to express and to experience, to know and to fulfill Who You Really Are, so that in the knowing you could show others who do *not* know.

That is your assignment. And you have given it to yourself.

And that is the great secret.

Are you ready to hear this secret? This is the secret which will change the world. This is the secret of why you have come here; of what you are doing in your body; of what the whole experience is all about.

Your job is to save others from every false thought they have about themselves; to show them who they really are by showing them who *you* really are. For they will not believe in themselves, and can only believe what they see in another. What they see in you, they may at last believe they can find in themelves. And so, by your life you re-mind people (that is to say, you cause them to be of a *new mind*) about Who They Really Are. This is the message you carry to them through your life lived. And that is what is meant by Concept #25.

CWG calls us *all* to be messengers. We are anyway, whether we want to be or not. As earlier noted, everything we think, say and do *sends a message to someone* about Who We Are. That message reaffirms to others Who They Are.

That's how it works here. We cannot be more collectively than we all are individually. And who are we individually? We don't know. We have forgotten. That's why we keep wandering around, as one who thirsts in the desert, reaching out to others, hoping they will affirm to us who we *think* we are, hoping they will *reflect* to us our highest notion of ourselves. When they do, we love them, for we've had our greatest thoughts about ourselves confirmed at last.

You see, we are trying everything we know (and every*one* we know) to *find ourselves*. This is not the recommended way to become Who You Really Are, but it is the way most are choosing.

And so we go around mirroring each other. We mirror each other and reaffirm each other in either our lowest thoughts about ourselves, or in our highest; in our smallest vision, or in our grandest.

Others know intuitively when they look at us that what they are seeing is a *mirror image of themselves*. Indeed, when others "like" us, it is because they see the best parts of themselves in us. When they "don't like" us, it is the "disliked" (and often the disowned) part of *themselves* from which they turn.

And so, we are creating together, most of us unconsciously. And our collective consciousness becomes our collective reality.

This is a powerful truth. Yet very few people understand this. And so, very few people understand their role – *the role they are playing right now* – in creating the world as we know it.

Are you, by your life, healing, saving? For that matter, have you ever decided *why* you've come here?

Try this on for size. It is a paraphrase from *A Course in Miracles*.

> *You have come to the room to heal the room.*
> *You have come to the space to heal the space.*
> *There is no other reason for you to be here.*

Does this sound "other"-centered to you, rather than "self"-centered? Then you have not yet moved to the grandest version of yourself, and the grandest purpose *for* yourself. When it is your purpose to be that which heals, then you are doing this for *you,* as an expression of Who You Really Are, not for another. The exterior result (healing of others) is the same. The interior reason is different. You have altered your *raison d'etre* – your *reason for being*.

EXERCISE

This is a process called Last Time/Next Time. In it, you are invited to look to see what you have been doing to "heal the space" through your life these days – and what you choose to do in the future. Take a moment in your study group to fill out the form below, then discuss (in smaller circles if your main group is too large) what the process brought up for you. If you are working in this Guidebook alone, reflect on this exercise in your journal.

LAST TIME / NEXT TIME

The last time someone cut me off on the highway without warning I. . .

The next time someone cuts me off on the highway without warning I will. . .

The last time I had a major disagreement with my spouse I. . .

The next time I have a major disagreement with my spouse I will. . .

The last time I was wrongly accused of something in public I. . .

The next time I am wrongly accused of something in public I will. . .

The last time I found I had been cheated by a friend I. . .

The next time I find I have been cheated by a friend I will. . .

The last time I learned my reservations have been given to someone else I. . .

The next time I learn my reservations have been given to someone else I will. . .

The last time I had a long talk with my parents I. . .

The next time I have a long talk with my parents I will. . .

The last time I entered a relationship I. . .

The next time, if I ever enter a relationship again, I will. . .

The last time I suddenly found my relationship ended I . . .

The next time, if I suddenly find my relationship ended, I will . . .

Further discussion: *A new pledge of troth; a new kind of promise*

We've concluded our game of *Last Time / Next Time* with a look at beginnings and endings of relationships because relationships are the most important aspects of our lives. It is through our relationship with God, our relationship with each other, and our relationship with every person, place, or thing on this planet that we are defined.

Are you in a "need-based" relationship right now? Do you "need" your loved one to be, do, or have some particular thing in order to continue loving them?

It has been said now several times that the difficulty in most romantic relationships is that most of us have been entering into them for the wrong reason. To end loneliness, stop depression, bring ourselves love, maybe even to improve our sex lives. In other words, we move into relationships to fill our needs and desires. We see a person across the room and we think, "Hmm, that person looks pretty good from over here," meaning that it appears as if they have the "stuff we want" and feel we need in order to be happy.

Now if that other person *does* turn out to have the "right stuff," we get closer to them. We may even marry them. In any event, we enter into a relationship with them based on *need fulfillment*. They, of course, are doing the same thing. And so we enter into an agreement. It is not unlike a compact between two nations. We have a trade agreement. I'll give you this if you'll give me that.

Yet on Valentine's Day we don't send a card which says, "I trade you very much." That is because we have decided to call this arrangement Love.

CWG sheds a lot of light on all of this. It also recommends that we never enter into a really meaningful relationship again unless we and our mate agree on purpose. Finally, it lists in one extraordinary paragraph what the purpose of relationship could be if we chose that.

This paragraph has come to mean a great deal to a great many people. Some have even written to me asking if they could use this paragraph as their wedding vow.

When I began creating this Guidebook I knew that I wanted to end its chapter on relationships with this paragraph, from page 141 of *CWG*, rewritten as a partnership commitment statement.

> To my beloved, with whom I now choose to be a partner in life: I agree at a conscious level that the purpose of my relationship with you is and will always be to create an opportunity, not an obligation — an opportunity for growth, for full self-expression, for lifting our lives to their highest potential, for healing every false thought or small idea we've ever had about ourselves, and for ultimate reunion with God through the communion of our two souls.

to pause and reflect

ASSIGNMENT:

This week, take stock. What is the most important relationship of your life? How have you been acting in that relationship? Have your actions spoken the highest idea you have about yourself? If there were some way you could speak an even higher idea, what would that look like? When would you choose to start?

Give yourself a week to think about this. Next week, in your journal, discuss these things. Come prepared to discuss them in your study group as well.

Additional Inquiries
from Chapter 8

1. What is the true function of relationships?
2. How does the typical couple's concerns in a relationship differ from the concerns God says would be for both parties' highest good?
3. Finding someone who loves you helps you to finally see, and love, yourself. *True or False?*
4. In truly loving relationship we put others first. *True or False?*
5. Our first and most important relationship should always be with:
    a. God
    b. our wisest teacher
    c. ourself
    d. the one who loves us most
6. When we reach Mastery we will react to attacks with love. Until then, what is the most appropriate way for us to react to hurts and attacks from others?
7. The highest thing we can do with our negative feelings is to have them. *True or False?*
8. A person who believes that life is about gains and losses believes he/she is a ______ .

9. A person who believes life is about loving or failing to love believes he/she is a _____ .

10. What is the Highest Choice when deciding who we are?

11. The best criterion for making the Highest Choice in any situation is:

   a. that which produces the highest good for you
   b. that which reflects God's wishes
   c. that which produces the highest good for another
   d. that which does the most good for all concerned

12. What is the first step in determining what is best for you in any situation?

13. Is war ever justified?

14. Can there be any spiritual purpose in declaring some things as evil?

15. What are the sacred obligations of marriage and life partnership?

16. We are born in sin and must be saved. *True or False?*

17. The length of a relationship is a measure of how successful it is. *True or False?*

18. If you and your partner would like to cultivate a long term relationship, what would be the best vow to make?

Chapter 9

You Are the Truth

Chapter 9 of *CWG* does not center itself around a particular topic, but rather, revisits some points made earlier in the text and introduces a few new ideas for our consideration. The most important point made in the chapter is summarized in dramatic fashion in the headline above. *You are the truth.*

What *CWG* is saying here, what God would like us to notice, is that in many areas of our lives we have given our power away. We have done this by making someone else's truth our own. This is so insidious that most of the time most of us don't even know it's happened. Yet the fact that we have done this is reflected in many of our most important choices and decisions.

TEXT REFERENCE:

And what, pray tell, forms the basis of your decision? Your own *experience*? No. In most cases you've chosen to accept someone *else's* decision. Someone who came before you and, presumably, knows better. . . *This is especially true on important matters. In fact, the more important the matter, the less likely you are to listen to your own experience, and the more ready you seem to be to make someone else's ideas your own.* — *Page 152*

As the book points out, many people have given up virtually total control over certain areas of their life because of this. Other people's opinions are more important than their own; other people's wisdom is greater than their own. Other people's sources are more authoritative than their own. And other people's truths are "more truthful" than their own. Yet this is the lie which others would have us believe. Many of the institutions in society *need* us to believe this lie, or they cannot get us to do what they need us to do to continue existing.

EXERCISE

Using an important topic (in this case, is killing "right" or "wrong"?), let's see how the state, how religions, and how all of society needs us to believe their truth in order to survive. Turn to page 153 in *CWG* and read aloud the material found there. When you have finished, please answer the three questions on the bottom of that page.

If you have successfully completed the exercise above, you have come to an inner awareness and have produced an outer experience of a great wisdom:

CONCEPT #26
You are the truth.

This is a very powerful statement. Because it is so powerful, it is to some very scary. Yet this statement in many ways summarizes the entire message of *CWG* – and if it is "scary," then *so must the whole book be.*

The statement YOU ARE THE TRUTH means there is no other truth which matters but your own. There is no absolute right and wrong. What is "right" is what you *say* is right. What is "wrong" is what you *say* is wrong. And by your decisions you paint a portrait of Who You Are. Indeed, by their decisions your states and nations have already painted such portraits. So, too, have your religions. So has your society.

Further discussion: *Life's biggest challenge; life's exciting adventure*

The biggest challenge you will ever face in your life – the grandest adventure you will ever take – will be the Definition of Your Self through the painting of this portrait.

What is important to remember about this portrait is that it can always change. What you put on the canvas today does not have to remain on the canvas tomorrow. You can paint over the image and create a new painting.

Would you like to create such a new painting right now? Good! Let us begin. Remember, just as your painting does not have to remain the same, so, too does it not have to change. Certain elements, certain colors chosen carefully from your palette, may remain exactly as they were, while in other areas of your portrait you may choose to alter some of the shades and hues.

Let's create an updated picture of Who You Are through the announcement of your latest decisions about what *you call* right and wrong.

EXERCISE

Below is a list of subjects. Next to each entry, simply make a check indicating whether you think it is right or wrong, or okay or not okay. Remember as you move through the list that YOU ARE THE TRUTH. Do not go to your memory bank to retrieve what someone else has told you about all of this. Just go inside and see what is true for you, right here, right now in your reality.

(*Note:* this is similar to an earlier exercise in which I asked you to say what you imagined God would think about various aspects of life. This time I am asking you what *you* think.)

(*Further Note:* I understand that you know there is no such thing as "right" and "wrong" in Ultimate Reality. What I am seeking to produce here is the experience of you creating what is "right" and "wrong" in YOUR reality, in order to thus define yourself as Who You Are.)

THE GAME OF 'RIGHT' AND 'WRONG'

THE ITEM	I CALL THIS "RIGHT" or "okay"	I CALL THIS "WRONG" or "not okay"
Prostitution		
Mixed marriage		
Gay marriage		
White lies which save face		
White lies which save another's face		
Using killing force to stop a killing		
Using killing force to make another accept your religion		

THE ITEM	**I CALL THIS "RIGHT" or "okay"**	**I CALL THIS "WRONG" or "not okay"**
Walking away from your spouse in the middle of an argument		
Gun control		
Abortion on demand		
Abortion to protect a mother's life or health		
Corporate 'welfare' (tax breaks to firms doing business a certain way)		
Individual welfare		
Premarital sexual encounters		
Intramarital sexual encounters		
Extramarital sexual encounters		
Extramarital sexual encounters with permission of spouse (in other words, Open Marriage)		
Corporal Punishment		
Medicinal use of marijuana		
Recreational use of marijuana		
Medicinal use of alcohol		
Recreational use of alcohol		
The death penalty		
Breaking the speed limit		
Physician-assisted suicide		
Loved one-assisted suicide		
Suicide		
Public assistance for legal aliens		

THE ITEM	I CALL THIS "RIGHT" or "okay"	I CALL THIS "WRONG" or "not okay"
Public assistance for illegal aliens		
Ebonics		
Cutting down old growth forests		
One world government		
Oral sex		
Setting prices at 5x your cost		
Setting prices at 3x your cost		
Setting prices at 100x your cost		
Getting the highest price you can get, irrespective of your cost		
Burning the American flag		
Gays in the military		
Finagling on your taxes		
Hazing rituals that cause physical pain		
Cloning animals to produce better stock		
Cloning humans to eliminate imperfections		
Using fetal cells from aborted embryos to halt or reverse Alzheimer's Disease		
Forcing all-male schools to accept females		
Boys & girls on high school wrestling teams		
Government subsidized health care		
The 'V' chip for parental TV control		
Sex education in schools		
Condom availability in schools		
Sexually explicit photographs, movies		

THE ITEM	I CALL THIS "RIGHT" (okay)	I CALL THIS "WRONG" (not okay)
VERY sexually explicit photos, movies		
Using profanity		
Using obscenities		
Living together outside of marriage		
Having children outside of marriage		
Refusing to rent to someone because of race		
Refusing to rent because of family size		
Refusing to rent for any reason, because it is your property and you should be able to do with it as you please		
Firing someone because of their sexual preference		
Refusing to hire someone because of their sexual preference		
Hiring, or refusing to hire, anyone you please because it is, after all, your business and you should be able to do as you wish		
Environmental protections which stop economic development		
Genetic engineering to eliminate disease		
Denying insurance on the basis of one's genetic predispositions		
Violent episodes on television		
Sexual episodes on television		

Further discussion: *The only game in town*

Now you may well ask yourself, why bother with all this? Why even start off on such a path of self-declaration and self-definition? What is to be gained by embarking on such a journey? Where is the incentive? What is the reason?

The answer is ridiculously simple.

There is nothing else to do.

As *CWG* carefully explains, this is the only game in town. In fact, you are playing this game right now – and always – whether you know it or not. **Everything you think, say, and do is an act of self-definition.**

Most of your life you have been defining yourself unconsciously – sometimes by unconsciously allowing yourself to imagine that you are what others have called you, that you are how others have imagined you. This is unconscious self-creation, as discussed on page 138 of this Guidebook. It is also self-creation without conscious decisions having been made beforehand as to Who and What You Choose to Be.

The book *Conversations with God*, and this handbook as well, issues an invitation for you to move to the next level, to step into *conscious* creation.

to pause and reflect

EXPERIMENT

This next week, see if you can avoid any "automatic" reactions which tend to create you as who you *were* rather than who you now choose to be.

Every time you see yourself falling into an old pattern, or moving into an old reaction to something, take just a second to stop and think: *Is this Who I Now Am?* If the answer comes up "yes," go ahead and be it. If the answer comes up "no," look to see who you *really are*, and then project that.

NOTE: If you fall into old patterns, don't "beat yourself up" about it. Just notice it and see whether it serves you to do that. If it doesn't serve you, decide not to fall into those patterns any more. Intend something else for yourself.

Remember, your life proceeds out of your intentions for it. Also remember, you are the truth.

Come to next week's group ready to discuss how the "truth that you are" feels to you. Does it feel good? Do you now choose a new truth? How has your work with *CWG*, Chapter 9, affected your life?

Additional Inquiries
from Chapter 9

1. You don't have to do anything. *True or False?*
2. Do we have an obligation to stop aggression?
3. What criterion is best to use in deciding whether killing another – or any other action – is justified?
4. Under what circumstances do you believe killing is justified?
5. When we don't have an answer in a moral dilemma it is appropriate to rely on a religious or spiritual authority. *True or False?*
6. Why struggle on a spiritual path to enlightenment if such a path is so arduous?
7. What is the inherent purpose of life?
8. It is arrogant to tell the universe your truth. *True or False?*

Chapter 10
Real Love Knows No Conditions

Of all the chapters in *CWG*, this is the one about which I receive the most mail. It seems to be many people's favorite.

I'm not surprised, really, because the directness and simplicity of its message is the Truth we have hoped to hear all of our lives. We love God, and God loves us. What could be more natural? What could be more perfect? What could be more comforting?

The implication of this message has even more impact than the message itself. For by its simplicity we receive the implication that God's love for us is unconditional. If there were conditions attached, God would have said so. He did not. Yet this kind of love is difficult for many people to believe in. Even coming from God. Perhaps *especially* coming from God.

TEXT REFERENCE:

You do not remember the experience of the love of God. And so you try to imagine what God's love must be like, based on what you see of love in the world. — *Page 17*

Yet God's love is not like the love we find in the world. Indeed, God's love is literally *out of this world.*

CONCEPT #27
God's love is unconditional.

Moving into Godliness means moving into unconditionality. The first step in that direction is making an accurate assessment of where you are today.

EXERCISE

Make a list below of the people for whom you have demonstrated unconditional love. (You love them no matter what they do; you have no expectations.)

1. ______________________________
2. ______________________________
3. ______________________________
4. ______________________________
5. ______________________________
6. ______________________________
7. ______________________________
8. ______________________________
9. ______________________________
10. ______________________________

Now make a list of the people who have demonstrated unconditional love for *you*.

1. ______________________________
2. ______________________________
3. ______________________________
4. ______________________________
5. ______________________________
6. ______________________________
7. ______________________________
8. ______________________________
9. ______________________________
10. ______________________________

to pause and reflect

ASSIGNMENT:

Make a list of the people to whom you choose to consciously show unconditional love this week. Include on the list at least three people to whom you can never remember demonstrating unconditional love and acceptance before. (The idea is to expand your circle!)

Answer these questions:

What would it take to show them this kind of love now?

What do you believe has stopped you before?

Does it seem as though it might be any easier this time?

If so, why? If not, why not?

Come prepared to discuss this with your study group next week. If you are working alone in this Guidebook, write a commentary at the end of this week in your journal. Be sure to answer the above questions.

Chapter 11
The Money Game

Few energies within the life experience affect us quite like money. Most people are very private about money – even more private than they are about their sex lives. Ask a person how many lovers they have had and many will tell you. (If they have had many, it could be a source of pride. If they have had very few, it could be a source of pride. Either way, they win!) Ask a person how many dollars they have or earn and many will feel uncomfortable. I believe this occurs because so many people have been damaged around the issue of money. They have been told that their value is tied up in how much they make; how much they are "worth."

People have been carrying around nonbeneficial thoughts about money for a long time. Most of these thoughts have been passed on from generation to generation. Here are some of the more common ones.

1. Money is bad.
2. People who *have* lots of money are bad.
3. Money doesn't grow on trees.
4. There is never enough money.
5. Money is the root of all evil.
6. It is easier for a camel to go through the eye of a needle than for a rich man to enter into the kingdom of heaven.
7. Money is dirty. It is "filthy lucre."
8. People who have lots of money are therefore "filthy rich."
9. Money is hard to come by.
10. You should never take money for a favor, or any "good thing."
11. Money talks.
12. Money corrupts.

With all these negative thoughts floating around it's a wonder anyone has any kind of good experience around money. Yet the truth is, nearly everyone's *experience* around having money has been good. And herein lies a contradiction. For our most frequent thoughts about money (it is bad) run counter to our most frequent experience of money (it's great to have it!). So we have to go around lying about our experience of money in order to justify our root thought about money.

Because of this inner contradiction, and our need to make our root thought about money "right," most of us push money away from ourselves. First we make it nearly impossible for us to get it (or certainly enough of it). Then, if and when we do get some, we make ourselves "disappear it" as fast as we can!

Sound familiar?

And even when we finally have enough, or more than enough, we then spend our time trying to make sure that we'll get to keep as much as possible as long as possible; that we don't lose any of it. So our worries about money hardly leave us when we have it. It is, in fact, an irony of life that in many cases the more money people have, the more people worry about money!

All of this comes out of our deepest root thought, or Sponsoring Thought, about money, which is that there simply isn't enough.

TEXT REFERENCE:

In fact, you have this root thought about just about everything. There's not enough money, there's not enough time, there's not enough love, there's not enough food, water, compassion in the world. . .whatever there is that's good, there's just *not enough*. — *Page 165*

This race consciousness of "not enough-ness" creates and recreates the world as you see it. It is time now to adopt a New Thought about all this. It's time to embrace a new, and to some a startling, concept.

CONCEPT #28
There's enough.

Those may just be the two most powerful words ever spoken.

I want you to read them again. Say them out loud.

If you are in a group, have each member of the group say them out loud. When the last person has done this, all of you say these words out loud together, in unison.

Do this now.

Good.

This one single truth – "There's *enough.*" – deeply understood and firmly held in consciousness, could change the world.

Think of it! What do you think would happen tomorrow if everyone on the planet – every person, every organization, every company, every government – operated from the simple truth that there is *enough.* There's enough time, there's enough money, there's enough love, there's enough food, there's enough of *everything we think we need in order to be happy.* There is enough to go around!

Now think about this. Really. *What do you think would happen if everyone operated from that?*

Well, you're right. If everybody simply came to each human encounter with that attitude, with that understanding, with that knowingness, those encounters would be less defensive, less devisive, less destructive. In fact, they would probably not be defensive, devisive, or destructive at all.

Everything we are fighting about on this planet has at its base the root thought that there is something of which there is not enough. (Even wars of religion and ethnicity are based in the thought that there are "not enough people who think as we do; not enough people like us!")

If only there was enough (of *whatever. . .*), our problem would be solved, right?

Well, the truth is, there *is* enough! And the proof is your own life. You want proof that there is "enough" of everything you need? *Notice that you're still here.*

Of course, some people are not still here. Some people have died because they did not have enough food, enough shelter, enough clothing. But that is not because there was not enough of these things to go around. Far from it. There was more than enough. Those people died because those who had *more* than enough refused, or could not find a way, to give of what they had to those who had none.

Lack of the will to *share* is the problem, not lack of the *stuff* to share.

My mother used to say, "Where there's a will, there's a way."

She was right.

If the world's people had the will to make certain that 400 humans did not die on this planet every hour from starvation, that would not happen. We would find a way to push through whatever political, cultural, behavioral, or physical barriers stand in our way, and we would *get the food to them.* Whatever the local government corruptions, whatever the number of rebels stopping food trucks as they drive from the airport, we would *get the job done.* It is absurd to accept the weakling excuse that a world which can send men to the moon cannot join with sufficient willpower to get food to everybody who needs it.

No, the issue is seldom that there is not enough "stuff" and almost always that there is not enough will.

Do *you* have the will? Do you currently tithe ten percent of everything you make to others?

EXERCISE

Take the following True/False test. This test is private. If you are working In a study group, take a moment to stop the group discussion and quietly complete this instrument.

1. I made $1200 or more last month, and gave $120 or more to my synagogue, temple, church, or other source of spiritual nourishment. *True* ____ *False* ____

2. I do not go to synagogue, temple, or church and cannot identify a "source of spiritual nourishment," but I gave $120 or more last month to a worthy charity or cause. *True* ____ *False* ____

3. I made less than $1200 last month, but nevertheless gave ten percent of all that I earned to church or charity. *True* ____ *False* ____

4. I spent $30 or more last month going to the movies, bowling, the theatre, out to dinner, or other entertainments, including rental movies at home, and gave an equal amount to those in need through programs in my community. *True* ____ *False* ____

5. I wrote a letter last month to my congressman or senator asking that this country increase its efforts (not necessarily its expenditures, but its efforts) to help the poor here and abroad. *True* ____ *False* ____

6. I am currently a sponsor in the Save The Children campaign or some other organization, giving $20 a month to feed a hungry child. *True* ____ *False* ____

7. When I pass a person asking for money on the street I always give them some, no judgments and no questions asked.
True ____ *False* ____

8. I see it as my personal responsibility to financially support programs which make mine a better community. *True* ____ *False* ____

9. I give as much each year to charity as I spend on my kids' sneakers and soccer league dues and equipment. If I smoke, I give the same amount to programs for the poor through my synagogue, temple, church, or other organization each month that I spend on tobacco.
True ____ *False* ____

10. I make sure when I file my income tax return each year that I give fully of my fair share, so that those who depend on publicly supported programs may continue to benefit from them.
True ____ *False* ____

Further discussion: *Turn around your life by turning around your values*

One of the chief reasons that more money doesn't flow into people's lives is that most people have their values reversed. Because they believe that money is "bad," they believe it is inappropriate to take money (especially large sums of money) for anything "good." Indeed, if a thing is judged very good by our society, it is usually valued *less* monetarily. So, as *CWG* says, "Your teachers make a pittance while your strip teasers make a fortune. Your leaders make so little compared to sports figures that they feel they have to steal to make up the difference. Your priests and rabbis live on bread and water while you throw coins at entertainers."

This "having it all backwards" produces a paradigm in which we insist that everything on which we place a high *intrinsic* value must *come cheaply*. In our mind the person who chooses the highest calling should receive the lowest pay. Thus we are scandalized when a minister or priest should happen to be driving a Cadillac. We pay puny wages to our research scientists fighting for a cure for AIDS, making them go begging for grants and government funding, while we support the giving of millions to someone for trying to hit a little white ball thrown by another from a mound of dirt. If he manages to hit the ball safely three times out of ten we offer him *zillions*.

What about you? What are *you* worth?

EXERCISE

Make a list of three things you do well, and the amount of financial reward you believe those skills are worth in today's market.

Three Things I Do Well:	What That is Worth:
1. ____________________	____________________
2. ____________________	____________________
3. ____________________	____________________

Now indicate on the lines below what you think each of these skills *should* be worth. Is it the same as you indicated above?

1. __________ 2. __________ 3. __________

What did the above exercise tell you? Do you believe you are overpaid or underpaid for the work that you do? Do you see yourself as being paid "just right"?

One of the mistakes many people make around money is thinking that the only way it can come to them is in return for some kind of work. The fact that this is not true for an impressive number of people does not diminish their belief in this system. The system holds that "we do stuff and we get money for it." This idea helps to create a whole new thought system around it which holds that "we are what we do."

This thought, too, is false, as we will see in the next chapter.

Right now, let's examine the first false thought.

Money does not come to us only in return for some kind of work. You know this, of course. And now you are going to prove it.

EXERCISE

Make a list below of as many ways as you can think of that money comes to people. Don't edit anything out. Just list the ways you can think of, without judgment. Use more paper if you need to.

Now go back and put a check mark next to every way which is acceptable to you; every way money comes to people which is okay with you.

Finally, go back once more and make an 'X' next to each of the acceptable ways money is coming to *you* now.

What percentage of the total number of acceptable ways is bringing money to *you* right now? Are you getting money 50% of the acceptable ways? 20%? What is your number? Write it in the space below.

____ %

> *What are you earning today? Can you see yourself demanding twice that amount? If not, why not? Is it that you are not worth it, or that the world will not pay it — which?*

What, if anything, does this tell you about your present potential for increasing the money flowing into your life? Discuss this now with your group, or write a statement about it in your journal.

All that is needed to reverse the fortunes in your life (if, indeed, you wish to do that) is to reverse your values around money, and the belief system they have sponsored.

In short, to turn your life around, turn your values around.

First, begin to value more *monetarily* those things which you value highly *intrinsically* — and *demonstrate that.* (The values you project will be the values projected onto you.)

Next, reverse your thought about what you believe your worth to be. No matter how much you value yourself — double it.

Then, choose to receive from the universe all that you are worth — but do not limit the universe to only one or two ways of getting you money. Do not make the mistake of connecting money inflow to work outflow. There is no connection — and the truly rich people know that.

to pause and reflect

EXPERIMENT

This week, choose to receive money from at least one unexpected source. Remember, it doesn't matter how much. It may be a quarter you find on the sidewalk, or $10,000 you discover you've inherited. It is not, and it is never, about amount. It is only about flow. So for your beginning experiment, simply make a mental choice – "I receive money from an unexpected source this week."

If you want to *really* get the flow moving, choose to *be* an "unexpected source" of money for another this week. (For several others if you can manage it.) *Give some money away.* It doesn't matter to whom, or why. Just give it away. You will find that you have started the flow. Now get ready for money to begin flowing to you. This is because you cannot give away that which you do not have – and so giving money to another is a dramatic statement to the universe of what you see yourself having. And the universe never denies you your picture of yourself.

Tell the study group next week about your experience. Share how long it took from your making the declaration above until the first unexpected money appeared in your life.

(There is no question that it will appear. Just watch for it, so that you don't miss it!)

Additional Inquiries
from Chapter 11

1. What are some typical blocks to abundance?
2. What is the best way to change your thought system?
3. Where do most of our thoughts and beliefs come from?
4. God's joy comes from our compliance with His wishes.
   True or False?

Chapter 12
Being vs. Doing

As we move through *CWG* toward its final chapters, we encounter some of the most important data in a book filled with extraordinary information. Chapter 12, in particular, contains at least three life-altering concepts. Concepts that shake the foundation of our present reality. For this reason, we've broken the chapter down into three sections in this Guidebook. Like Chapter One, there is far too much material here to be taken in one gulp.

The three paradigm shifting concepts in *CWG*, Chapter 12, any *one* of which could remake your entire experience of life if applied daily, are:

1. You are a human being.

2. To want something is to push it away from you.

3. Your life has nothing to do with your body.

Now it sounds almost silly to say that the first of these concepts is profound. Yet its implications are enormous, and its meaning is only partially grasped by all but the most advanced among us.

In the *CWG* dialogue this concept was introduced within the context of some additional considerations about money. God's no dummy. He knows how to get our attention, and how to make immutable wisdom stick by applying it to practical everyday problems. And there is no problem more practical or more "everyday" than the problem of money.

For most people, money *is* a problem. That is true for the vast majority of people on this planet. For them, it is a constant challenge. Perhaps you have moved past this challenge. Perhaps you have mastered "the money game." If so, you are among the minority. You are a member of a very small group. Even so, keep reading ahead. You can use this information to help others.

Probably the biggest misunderstanding I have encountered over and over again in people trying to figure out "the money game" is their thought about how it is that money comes to us. What makes money flow to us? How does it come to pass that another willingly gives us this stuff?

Most people believe (as noted in the last chapter) that money comes to them in exchange for something they do. In this construction they see a *quid pro quo*. They give this, and they'll get that.

In truth, the arrival of money (and all good things) has nothing to do with what we're doing. It just *looks* that way. (And, I will admit, sometimes those appearances can be very convincing.)

Chapter 12 in *CWG* lays out a new thought system about all this. A thought system which suggests that it is what you are *being* which attracts to you the various experiences of your life (including the experience of financial abundance), not what you are *doing*.

TEXT REFERENCE:

If you think your life is about doingness, you do not understand what you are about. Your soul doesn't care *what* you do for a living — and when your life is over, neither will you. Your soul cares only about what you're *being* while you're doing *whatever* you're doing. It is a state of beingness the soul is after, not a state of doingness. – *Page 170*

This is the job of the soul – and hence, your job, your "mission," your *purpose* on this planet and in this life. You are here to "be" something, not to "do" something. (It is through this "beingness" that you will "SAVE" (wake up) others. (See page 138.)

CONCEPT #29
You are a human being.

Be assured that this is more than a simple aphorism. In this statement is an enormous Truth. A truth that could change your life forever.

Many people imagine that the way to get to "beingness" (that is, to "be" happy, to "be" secure, to "be" peace, is to *do* certain things). It is a fact, for sure, that *everything we do is an attempt to achieve a State of Beingness*. With every action we are attempting to achieve a state of being. Did you know that? Have you ever thought of it this way? It is true.

Let me explain further.

Everything you do, you do for a *reason*. There is an *anticipated outcome*. This outcome has to do in almost every case with a phenomenon I have come to call "Havingness." That is to say, most of the things we do we do because we *hope to get something out of it*. There is something, when all is said and done, that we hope to "have" as a result of all this.

Now some people have a very difficult time admitting this. That's because they live within a belief system which suggests that "getting" and "having" is "bad," and that we should therefore "do" stuff not because it enures to our own personal benefit, but for some higher reason. This they call "selfless giving."

In truth, there is *no such thing as selfless giving*. There is *no such thing as a selfless act*. Even the act of doing something selflessly is a *selfish* act, for it allows us to feel that we are doing something selflessly, and that is a good feeling. We "feel good about ourselves." Which, by the way, *is totally okay*.

> *Can you think of a time when you were told not to feel so good about yourself? Who told you that? What was their reason?*

I emphasize this because there are some who insist it is "wrong" to feel good about oneself. It is the ego exerting undue influence on us. It is this. It is that. It is Satan, for heaven sake. In truth, it is none of these. Feeling good about yourself is *all you are trying to do here*. Because what you *are* is "good." You are, in realilty, "that which is good." And all you are trying to do in your life is *experience yourself* as *exactly Who You Are*.

(The remarkable and poignant statement in *CWG* about Who You Are, which is reproduced on page 97 of this Guidebook, should be read daily as a reminder of what God has to say about you.)

Let's be clear, then, that not only are there no selfless acts – no acts were ever *intended* to be selfless. Indeed, the whole *point of action itself* is to *produce an experience of the Self*.

Most people do not visualize it this way. They do not see what is actually going on. In most people's understanding, they are doing things in order to "get" things, and after they "have" those things, they think they will "be" something.

Perhaps they will be "happy." Or perhaps they will be "secure." Or perhaps they will be, finally, "at peace." These "states of beingness" are what they imagine will proceed from their having what they got by doing all they did!

Got it?

Good, because this is hard to follow.

Now, if you don't believe this theory of human behavior is correct (or if you'd like proof that it is), do the following exercise.

EXERCISE

Make an analysis of why you "do" certain things. Using the form below, list in Column 2 what you imagine you will "get" out of the common, everyday "doingness" experiences shown in Column 1. Then list in Column 3 how you think you will feel after getting what you've listed in Column 2.

(I've made the first several entries here from my own experience to give you an example of how this exercise is done.)

A THING I DO COMMONLY	WHAT I THINK I WILL "GET" WHEN I DO THIS	WHAT I WILL "BE" (FEEL) WHEN I GET THIS
Go to work every day	a paycheck	secure
Call my wife if I'm going to be late	my wife's thanks and approval	happy
Use my turn signals	where I'm going without injury	safe
Your turn. . .		

For many people all of life is a process of *doing* something in order to *have* something in order to *be* something. In this they have the Be-Do-Have paradigm reversed. They are trying to arrive at a state of beingness by moving into doingness. Yet the creative process works best the other way around. First decide what to "be" (that is, what state of beingness you wish to experience), then move into that beingness without doing anything.

(In my lectures I am fond of saying, "You don't have to do a damned thing. In fact, you should *stop* doing 'damned things.' Until you do, very little will work out for you, and you'll walk around muttering, 'Well, I'll be damned'.")

Out of this beingness you will find that doingness will flow. Indeed, beingness fully experienced will *produce* doingness. And that doingness will be a reflection of the beingness which gave it birth.

Let me explain.

A person can either *do* something in order to "be happy," or a person can start the day by simply deciding to "be happy," and the things that person will *do* will automatically reflect that. You can either use doingness as a means of *getting* to beingness – or you can decide to *"already be there" – and let your doingness be a demonstration of that.*

Let's just try an experiment in your mind. Ask yourself this: if I simply decided, arbitrarily and as a result of nothing in particular, to "be happy" for the next hour or so, would it change in any way the things I say and do during that time?

Let's choose some other states of beingness. Supposed you decided, just because you thought it might be fun, to be seductive; to be sensual. Do you think you might speak and act any differently than you normally do? How about compassion? Do you think you could arbitrarily decide to "be compassionate"? And if you did, do you think it would change in any way the manner in which you behave, even for a short time? Of course it would. In every case it would.

The fact of the matter is (and this is one of the great secrets of life) you can choose to *be* in any state of beingness you wish, and you can *choose this ahead of time.* Your experience of *how you are being* does not have to be a reaction to what is going on around you. Quite to the contrary, what is going on around you can be a result of *how you are being.*

When you learn this, you begin to turn life upside down. You no longer react to situations, you create them. You move *from* a state of beingness, rather than trying to move *into* a state of beingness. There is a vast difference.

to pause and reflect

ASSIGNMENT:

Draw up a simple chart made up of seven squares running horizontally across a page. Label the squares S M T W TH F SA.

Now pick seven "states of being" (any seven which appeal to you) and write a state of being ("happy," "sensual," "compassionate," etc.) in each square.

Decide that each day during the coming week, you are going to choose ahead of time to "be" whatever you have written in that day's square. "Do" whatever it takes to "be" that. Keep your beingness decision fresh in your mind throughout the day by leaving little notes to yourself, little reminders, all over the place, ("Be HAPPY." "Be SENSUAL." "Be SECURE," etc.)

Work hard at this. **Do not do anything** *which takes you away from your state of beingness for the day.*

Keep a log of your experiences, and each night make detailed notes of how your day went, and how many times you consciously experienced yourself being what you chose to be ahead of time.

This is called Conscious Creation.

You are literally creating your ***self****. Or, more accurately,* ***re-creating yourself anew.***

Do not be surprised if you experience this as the breakthrough moment of your life.

Chapter 12, Section 2
Want not, waste not

God says you may not have anything you want.

Now that may not be an easy statement to swallow, but it is the truth.

TEXT REFERENCE:

Remember, you cannot have what you want, but you may experience whatever you have. – *Page 176*

The statement is founded on an even larger truth, covered in Concept #3 of this Guidebook. Please go back to page 41 and review that Concept if you do not remember what it is.

If, at each of the three levels of creation, you are residing in a space of "wanting" something, *you may not have it.* This is because. . .

CONCEPT #30
To want something is to push it away from you.

How can this be true? How can God invite us to call upon Him whenever we are in need if this is so?

It is quite simple, and there are no contradictions here. We begin our understanding by remembering that your thought is creative, your word is creative, and your actions are creative. Indeed, your actions are creations in and of themselves, and serve to produce other creations.

Now if your thought about something (let's use money as our example here) is that you "want" it, and if your words about this speak of "wanting" it, and if you act as if this is something that you "want" – then the universe has no choice but to give you the experience you have called forth. . .namely, the *experience of wanting it.*

The universe, you see, is a great big xerox machine. Like a photocopier, it does not make judgments about what you put into it. It simply duplicates it.

Think of it this way: this particular copying machine is computerized. And the word "I" is the access code. "I" opens the program. Whatever you say following "I" (or "I am") is like a computer command. It tells the program what to do. And in this case the program is called "CREATION."

There is another way I like to use to help people truly understand the power of their thoughts, words, and actions. I say to them: "You are always praying."

They say, "What?"

And I repeat, "You are *always praying.*"

Think of it. Imagine it. How would you feel, what would you change, if you lived within a paradigm which announced that every thought, word, and deed is a prayer?

Your statements are your requests. So if you say *"I want money,"* and if you say it often enough, you will get exactly that. You will find yourself *wanting money.*

To put this yet another way, think of it as self-description. When you use the word "I" you are just describing yourself, and what is true for you. The universe has no choice but to agree with your description, and produce that in your reality.

For all the reasons above, I can say without equivocation: *Never ask God for anything.*

Thank God instead.

The greatest prayer is a prayer of thanksgiving.

The Master is one who is grateful *in advance* for that which is chosen. A Master does not "want," *ever.* For a Master knows that to want something is to waste it. That is to say, you will waste the fact that *you already have it.*

> *When was the last time you prayed? Was it a prayer of asking, or of thanksgiving?*

God says in *CWG* that we already have everything we could ever want. This is not new information. It has come from other sources as well. ("Even before you ask, I will have answered.") In *CWG - Book 2* it is explained that there is no such thing as Time, only the Eternal Moment of Now. Therefore, everything you have ever had, or ever will have, you *have right now.* You simply don't know it. You are not aware of it. You are not conscious of its being there.

You are walking around unconscious.

Masters do not walk around unconscious. Masters are consciously aware that whatever they choose is already given them, already present. It is simply a matter of enlarging one's consciousness to experience that. So a Master *always* prays a prayer of thanks. *Gratitude. . .*says the Master. . . *is the attitude.*

A Course in Miracles inspired me to use the most powerful prayer I have ever heard.

"Thank you, God, for helping me to understand
that this problem has already been solved for me."

Have you ever heard a more powerful prayer? I think not.

The work of the student who would seek mastery is to change attitude. This means changing every thought, word, and deed.

As a start, try the exercise below.

EXERCISE

Here is a chart with a list of topics covering many aspects of life as a human being. Beneath each topic is a statement often heard from people about that subject. In the space beneath the statement, write a new statement which more closely reflects the truth which has been presented here.

TOPIC: Money	A STATEMENT OFTEN HEARD ABOUT THIS TOPIC: *"I need more money in my life, and I want it right now."*

A NEW STATEMENT ABOUT THIS TOPIC WHICH EMBODIES THE TRUTH I NOW KNOW:

TOPIC: Sex	A STATEMENT OFTEN HEARD ABOUT THIS TOPIC: *"I wish I had more sex in my life. I want more romance."*

A NEW STATEMENT ABOUT THIS TOPIC WHICH EMBODIES THE TRUTH I NOW KNOW:

TOPIC: Love	A STATEMENT OFTEN HEARD ABOUT THIS TOPIC: *"I want someone to love in my life! Someone who will love me. Is that so much to ask?"*

A NEW STATEMENT ABOUT THIS TOPIC WHICH EMBODIES THE TRUTH I NOW KNOW:

TOPIC: God	A STATEMENT OFTEN HEARD ABOUT THIS TOPIC: *"I'm not even sure I believe in God. Why doesn't He answer my prayers?"*

A NEW STATEMENT ABOUT THIS TOPIC WHICH EMBODIES THE TRUTH I NOW KNOW:

You may want to continue this exercise (in fact, we suggest that you do) by coming up with at least six other topics (and more if you've got them) and filling in the larger two boxes for each. Brainstorm in your study group to pick topics and to decide on an "often heard statement." Then have each member create their own "new statement about this topic." Share these new thoughts in the group.

If you are working alone, create some of the above forms in your journal and pick more topics about which you'd like to move into a new thought.

This is the *New Thought Movement* you've heard so much about. Now you know what it's really *all about!*

Further discussion: *Why "Affirmations" seldom work*

By now you may have concluded that all we have done here is create a series of affirmations. Well, perhaps. Yet these "affirmations" differ from the affirmations used by most people in the New Thought Movement, from my observation.

If I have heard it once, I have heard it a thousand times. "My affirmations don't work! I do them and do them and do them, and they don't work. I think them, I write them, I speak them, but they just don't work." There is a reason for this. Affirmations seldom work when they are announcements of what we want to be so. They almost always work when they are declarations of what is *already* so. And you must *believe* that it is already so.

No, you must not believe it. You must *know it.* Knowing and believing are not the same thing. "Knowing" requires a level of faith far above anything ever involved in "believing." You can "believe" a thing, and that is good. But if you absolutely "know" a thing, that is infinitely better. One can step off a ledge believing one will not fall, and one can step off a ledge *knowing* one will not fall. There is a quantum difference. It is a *felt* difference.

Have you used affirmations in your life? If so, do you think they work? What do you think of the ideas presented here?

With belief there is always doubt. At least a tiny bit of doubt. That is why we call it a "belief." With knowing, all doubt is erased. There is *no doubt about it.*

Over and over again I have seen people working with affirmations such as "I am rich beyond my wildest dreams," or "I have my perfect mate." Sometimes teachers even tell students to put a date to the affirmation, as in, "I will find my perfect mate by June."

The problem is, you must *know* that the statement is *true for you now* in order for the affirmation to be effective. And many people cannot move to a level of awareness sufficient to see the truth in statements such as, "I am rich beyond my wildest dreams." They make such an affirmation and their mind shouts, "The hell you say!"

So here is a trick. Use affirmations which declare what you can accept as true for you now. As you see these affirmations manifesting in your life, you will expand your "ability to know." Then you will know even larger truths. And larger. And even larger still. Soon you will become *a real Know-It-All!*

Using one of the issues above, here is an affirmation, a "new thought," which most people can move into without doubting: "My perfect mate is coming to me now."

You may think this is just playing with words, but I want you to know that such a small twist in the verbiage has done more than simply change words. It has changed lives.

And yes, I am aware of the argument that this is a weak affirmation, because if we keep saying it, then we will create our perfect mate as always being "on the way" and never *arriving*. But when working with New Thought in this way, we must always begin where we are; start with what we can accept. If a person can accept this perfect mate is on the way, that produces a whole new mindset, which can create a whole new reality. Trust me. I have seen it work.

to pause and reflect

ASSIGNMENT:

This week think about what you are thinking. Say something about what you are saying. Do something about what you are doing. Know and understand that your thoughts, words, and actions do create your reality.

Keep a running log, in writing, of how you think, speak, and act this week. Make up this log by subject matter. Pick out ten subjects that swirl around your life. Then, for each of the next seven days, notice what you are creating with regard to these aspects of your experience. Keep close track.

Report to your study group next week, or, if you are working through this Guidebook alone, make an important entry in your journal seven days from now.

Chapter 12, Section 3
You're nobody

It is interesting that millions of parents in this world work like the devil in the hope that their children can one day "be somebody." There is no devil, of course, but if there were, this is exactly what he would want us to do. So here is some advice. Work like a *God*, so that one day your children can be *nobody*.

There is not a single idea more destructive to the human race than the idea that we are our bodies. If you think you are your body you will make all kinds of choices, selections, and decisions which will produce little or no benefit to you. Perhaps you've already noticed this.

The seemingly inexorable desecration of our planet, the wars which have killed millions upon millions through the centuries, the indignities, humilities, and actual pain suffered by people every day the world over – all of this is due to one massive misundstanding. We think we are our bodies.

Nothing could be further from the truth. And living such a thought places *us* further and further from the truth. It places the entire human race as far from the truth as it could possibly be. Such a life has nothing to do with reality. It is unreal.

Have you ever said to yourself when reading the newspaper or watching the horrors of the nightly news on television, "Man, this is *unreal. . .*" ?

> *What part of your body are you most proud of? What part are you least proud of? Do you like your body?*

Well, you're right. It is. And the challenge facing humankind as it moves through the last part of the 20th century and into the New Millennium is whether we intend to "get real," or keep making the same choices and producing the same results.

It is difficult not to identify with your body. After all, this is "you." At least it sure *seems* as though this is "you." It is the only "you" which you have ever known, that's for sure.

Or is it?

Have you ever known "another" you? Have you ever in your life felt you'd gotten in touch with another part of yourself? How would you describe that part? What did it feel like?

However it felt, if you've ever had this experience you may not be quite so sure that this body of yours *is* Who You Really Are. In fact, quite to the contrary. You may now feel very sure that it is *not*.

Those who have had such transcendental experiences (we are said to "transcend" the body in such moments) often change their whole way of living as a result.

TEXT REFERENCE:

There comes a time in the evolution of every soul when the chief concern is no longer the survival of the physical body, but the growth of the spirit; no longer the attainment of worldly success, but the realization of Self. – *Page 180*

Actually, your life is not about what your body is doing. . .yet what your body is doing is a reflection of what your life is about.

This is another way of saying that your body *shows everyone* what your life is about, but your life is not about what your body does. Your life is about what you are. And what you become. And what you have become is *in evidence* in everything the body does.

I will say it again. Your life is about what *you are*. And you are a great deal more than your body. You are your body, your mind, and your soul; a combination of all three. What your body is doing day to day is an *indication* of what that combination is – not the *creator* of it.

And so we come to another wisdom of life-altering proportions.

CONCEPT #31
Your life is not about your body.

This is an incredible statement. And particularly since the largest number of people alive think that life *is* about the body, its implications are staggering.

Most people create entire life scenarios based on their thought that they are their body. Major decisions are made, choices are implemented which people hope and believe will bring benefit, succor, protection, comfort, and yes, physical satisfaction and happiness, to their body, and the bodies of those they love.

If we thought we were not our bodies, where would that leave us? What reason would we have to be, do or have anything? That's a very good question. It is a question *CWG* encourages us to explore.

If we explore it deeply enough we will discover that the answer is this: we would be a thing, we would do a thing, we would choose to have a thing not because of what benefit we felt it might be to our body, but because of what benefit it might be to our soul.

We would see each act as an act of self-definition. We would select or reject an act, a word, a thought based on our idea about ourselves and how well the thought, word or act advanced that idea. We would see each of life's rapidly presenting options as being either in harmony or in disharmony with Who We Are and who we Choose To Be, and we would then simply have to decide whether we really choose to be that, or just say that we do.

EXERCISE

Accept for the moment that the above concept is true, literally. If your life did not need to have anything to do with your body, or pleasing, caring for, or protecting the body of another, what — if anything — would change in the way you live?

WITH REGARD TO MY. . .	HERE IS WHAT WOULD CHANGE
. . .marriage, or my experience of romantic partnership	
. . .job, or my experience of career and 'right livelihood'	
. . .lifestyle, or my experience of environment, personal activities, and friendships	

WITH REGARD TO MY. . .	HERE IS WHAT WOULD CHANGE
. . .hobbies, or my experience of myself in my leisure time	
. . .money, or my experience of how I spend what I make, and on what	
. . .sexuality, or my experience of my sensual self	
. . .spirituality, or my experience of my Higher Self	

Feel free to extend this list if you like, adding items that allow you to look more deeply into yourself.

Further discussion: *Going off the deep end*

Freeing as this kind of information, and exercise, may be, it is important not to take it too far. *CWG* warns against this kind of overreaction (see page180-81). Tempting as it may be to ignore matters of the body once one realizes that one's life has nothing to do with the body, it would be wasteful to fail to take care of the body. It would not be an honoring of the Temple of your Being. Honor this temple, honor your body – simply do not build your life and all of your decisions around it.

What have you done to honor the Temple of your Being today?

If you make all of your daily choices and decisions based on what it does for your body, you will wind up spending many years engaged in activities – what I call "doingness" – having nothing to do with your soul. Your soul will feel empty. You will wonder what your life has been all about.

The interesting thing about this is that no one else will care, no one is keeping score, no one is watching. No one even has a judgment about how it all turns out. Not even God.

In the end, it's just us and our Selves. Just us and Us.

And it is when we let ourselves down, when we pay attention to body-doingness only, with no focus on the larger aspects of life, that we create the most emptiness in our life – and the most disappointment.

The irony of all this is that we are doing it to ourselves. It is as the late cartoonist Walt Kelly observed through the voice of his deliciously wry character *Pogo*:

"We have met the enemy, and they is us."

to pause and reflect

EXPERIMENT

Let's try a lab experiment this week. When you have a choice to make in the coming seven days, no matter what that choice is about (something as simple as what to have for lunch, or as complex as what to do next in your relationship or at your job), see if you can bring to mind first, before you make any moves or announcements, your grandest idea about yourself. Then measure your current options against that idea, and see if any of them fit.

See how often you can do this during the week, and in what way, if at all, it impacts your decision-making process.

Bring the results of your experiment to the study group next time, or write them in your journal.

Additional Inquiries
from Chapter 12

1. What are the sources of "doing" and "being"?
2. The human soul is seeking to be God. *True or False?*
3. Sometimes in life "bad" things happen to you that are not in your best interest. *True or False?*
4. What are the roles of the soul, the mind and the body in our earthly experience?
5. While it may not be the most enlightened way, obedience to God will produce salvation. *True or False?*
6. When does the soul achieve its goal of finally "knowing itself in its own experience"?
7. God says that as creative beings we can have anything we want. *True or False?*
8. What thought or attitude will bring our desires into reality?
9. At the time of what we call our death, we drop the body, but remain alive in our soul. *True or False?*
10. Through all our many lifetimes the blueprint (original idea) of Who We Really Are is held by __________ .
11. God's only judgment about our life comes after our death. *True or False?*
12. What things do we need to do to be truly happy?
13. It is spiritually inappropriate to insist on doing work or other activity which enhances your soul if that results in a reduced quality of life for your dependents. *True or False?*

Chapter 13
Just For the Health of It

I must admit I wouldn't have predicted it, but. . .one of the most controversial parts of *Conversations with God - Book 1* was, after all was said and done, the chapter on *health*.

We must all be pretty attached to our vices, because of the very few letters of disagreement I received on the book (less than 100 letters out of 6,000 received to date have been negative), more focused on these sections than any other passage. . .and this is a book filled with some fairly outrageous stuff.

The drinking of alcohol, in particular, must be a favorite activity among human beings, judging from the readers' response to *CWG's* pronouncement on this subject. And just what was the inflammatory statement which caused all the uproar?

TEXT REFERENCE:

The body was not meant to intake alcohol. It impairs the mind. – *Page 191*

Of all that was written in this manuscript, I would have thought that statement to be among the most benign. So there you have it. As a population, we're pretty attached to our booze. We like our red meat, too, and both are killing us. Yet if that isn't sufficient to do the job, millions of us will guarantee the result with tobacco.

Some of *you*, reading this Guidebook right now, are probably doing all three.

Now there's nothing "wrong" with this. "Right" and "wrong" are judgments, not realities. We've already established that. Just be honest enough to admit what you're doing. Step out of denial and into truth. Tell your loved ones straight up, "Look, I know this stuff is not doing me any good, but, you see, I am a wimp and a weakling and I can't stop myself." Or, if that is not how you see yourself, then say, "Actually, I am not a weakling, and I *can* stop this. I just don't choose to. I know all this stuff may even shorten my life, but, you see, I don't care. And I know that you care, because you love me and want me around as long as you can have me, but I obviously don't care about that, either."

Or, if *that* is not your truth, you can always retreat into the New Age Protection Zone. You can say, "My thought creates my reality, and my thought is that this stuff won't hurt me."

Aside from the fact that there are very few beings presently on the planet whose individual thought-power has been demonstrated to be greater than the co-creative power of collective consciousness, this argument should fly.

It is ironic that while most people choose to cling tenaciously to their own downfalls, one of the most difficult things for many to accept about human health is that each of us is responsible in the matter. Bad health is not something that happens *to* us, it happens *because* of us. (The same is true of good health, of course.)

There are a thousand and one ways this cause-and-effect relationship plays itself out in our lives – which is what makes it so difficult to *see* the relationship, much less fully understand it.

Precisely because there are so many intertwinings in the fabric of our experience, it becomes nearly impossible to follow the thread from Point A to Point B – from this Cause to that Effect – when it comes to our health. And as soon as we *do* come up with evidence from our science labs that such and such behavior causes damage to the human organism, a chorus of nay-sayers rises up to poo-poo it.

So, yes, it is difficult for us to see the part we have played in creating the illnesses with which we have been afflicted. Yet this doesn't make it any less true that. . .

CONCEPT #32
Your health is your creation.

Most people cannot see themselves as creative, or responsible for, the condition with which they've just been diagnosed, or the heart attack they had last year, or even the headache they've just acquired, much less more exotic diseases such as atherosclerosis or Parkinson's or Altzheimer's. How does a little child participate in the creation of her own debilitating muscular dystrophy?

That's a fair question. We're pretty sure she didn't willfully call it upon herself. It was not an act of conscious choice. Does that mean it was unconscious?

Yes.

In the sense that "unconscious" can mean that which is not done deliberately, that which was not intentional at the conscious human level, yes. . .this choice was "unconscious."

There is no way for us to know the individual path of another soul. It is not part of the plan for us to be aware of the purpose and intentions of another spirit as it once again takes on physical form. But this much we do know. Nothing – not a single thing – happens in God's world which is not with good reason. Everything which occurs in the incarnation experience of an individual soul occurs at the *behest* of that soul, as a result of the *creations* of that soul, or of the *co-creations* in which it has engaged with others – what might be called the creations of the Collective Consciousness. (This creates a large part of our reality.) Either way, *CWG* leaves no room for doubt. It makes its statement on this subject clearly and without equivocation.

TEXT REFERENCE:

. . .all illness is self created. Even conventional medical doctors are now seeing how people make themselves sick. Most people do so quite unconsciously. . .so when they get sick, they don't know what hit them. It feels as though something has befallen them, rather than that they did something to themselves. – *Page 187*

So yes, we create our own health (consciously or unconsciously) from the earliest moments of our life to the last. We are creating both collectively and individually, with each level of creation playing its effect on the overall experience we call life.

If your consciousness is high enough to overcome individually the cumulative effects of the collective creations of humankind, or what you have been *told* will happen, then you *can* act with impunity in what you eat, what you drink, what you do with your life. You will not be damaged or harmed. The "new ager's" after all have it right. It is just a matter of consciousness.

So let's see where your consciousness lies – by your own assessment. (No one else's matters.) Take the test below.

EXERCISE

Give yourself five minutes to complete the following self-evaluation instrument.

Self Evaluation of Consciousness

1. On a scale of 1-10 (and understanding that these things fluctuate from moment to moment), I observe my spiritual awareness and consciousness to be, most of the time, at a level of _____.

2. This level is sufficient to overcome the negative effects of the collective consciousness and the co-creations of those around me. *True* ___ *False* ___

3. I believe and know that — because of my present consciousness about it — I can ward off any negative effect, impact, or damage to my physical organism which others claim might result from the following activities *(check those you feel sure about)* :

___ Smoking ___ Drinking ___ Eating red meat
___ Using marijuana ___ Mainlining cocaine
___ Unprotected sex with a stranger ___ Fast driving
___ Fatty foods ___ Jumping off buildings

4. I am an Immortalist and know I have the ability to live in my present physical body as long as I wish, without limitation. *True* ___ *False* ___

5. If I *am* confronted in the future with an undesireable health condition, I feel I am now of sufficient consciousness to affect a spontaneous healing of those conditions I have checked below:

___ Headache ___ Toothache ___ Lung cancer
___ Influenza ___ Indigestion ___ Heart attack
___ Sexually transmitted diseases ___ Leukemia
___ Ulcers ___ Colon cancer ___ Hemorrhoids
___ Any disease or illness

6. There is no reason to change any of my behaviors because my consciousness creates my reality, and in my reality I will never be sick as a result of anything I eat, drink, or do. *True* ___ *False* ___

7. My past experience supports the above statement. *True* ___ *False* ___

Further discussion: *Changing your life, extending your life*

It takes a great deal of determination to change one's life. Most of us have not demonstrated that level of willingness in the past.

That doesn't mean we can't start tomorrow. It is also true that it is not necessary to do so.

The above test gives you an idea of where your consciousness lies with regard to this item in your life called health. If you feel that your consciousness is not yet sufficiently developed to overcome any unwanted outcome or condition, it may be useful now for you to explore some health alternatives which could serve you in the years ahead.

EXERCISE

Have a round table discussion of this whole health question now with your study group. You may want to read the first few pages of *CWG*, Chapter 13, aloud, having one person read my words and others read the responses I received. Read from the beginning of the chapter to the bottom of page 193. That should take only about 15 minutes. How does the information here square with your own belief system? How does it differ?

What impact, if any, does this information have on your ideas about your future? What impact do you choose for it to have?

If you are working alone with this Guidebook, do the reading aloud as suggested (you may even want to record it), then answer the above questions in your journal. (Here again it is suggested that you may find the already recorded audio book of *CWG* most helpful.)

to pause and reflect

ASSIGNMENT:

During the coming week take an inventory of your healthy (and unhealthy) behaviors, using the form below. Bring your results to next week's group for discussion, or place them in your Journal.

My Health Behaviors Inventory:

1. At present I would describe my overall health as. . .
___ good ___ fair ___ not good ___ bad

2. Here is a look at some of the behaviors I exhibit over a seven-day period, together with my assessment of whether those behaviors are beneficial (marked with a "B"), or non-beneficial (marked with an "N"). *(Your assessment will, of course, be based on where your consciousness is about these things, whether you believe you have overcome Collective Consciousness, etc.)*

MONDAY	TUESDAY	WEDNESDAY

THURSDAY	FRIDAY	SATURDAY

SUNDAY

If these forms do not provide you with enough room, please use any form of diary which works best for you.

The idea is for you to simply keep track of what you are feeding, and doing with, your physical form over 7 days, placing a "B" or an "N" after each entry.

At the end of the week, add up the total number of entries, then figure the percentage of "B" entries and the percentage of "N" entries.

Share this with your study group.

Chapter 13, Section 2
Your true relationship with God

The second half of *CWG,* Chapter 13, opens doors onto the most important question of all time. What is our true relationship with God?

From the beginning of time human beings have sought to know more about that relationship, or if such a relationship even existed. For centuries it has been our religions which have sought to unravel this mystery for us, but all they have done is create more mystery. They have generated more questions than answers, more taboos than revelations, more fear of God than love of God.

TEXT REFERENCE:

Religion is your attempt to speak of the unspeakable. It does not do a very good job. – *Page 195*

Most of us in today's culture have been affected by religion in one way or another, even if we've never belonged to one. At this point in your study of the *CWG* material, let's take a look at what your experience of religion has been.

EXERCISE

Fill out the chart below.

My religious experience
as a child was:

This led to the following conception of God:

. . .which in turn produced this relationship with God:

. . .as a result, here are the main things religion has taught me:

1.

2.

3.

4.

5.

6.

7.

The revelations in Chapter 13 create an opportunity to form a new relationship with God which may be more functional than any you have previously experienced. This relationship will be soundly based in. . .

CONCEPT #33
You are the body of God.

This revelation astounds the mind, for most of us cannot conceive of ourselves in this way. Once again, re-reading the material in the actual manuscript is recommended here, for this material will allow you to experience, better than anything which could be written here, the full implication of what came through in this portion of the dialogue.

EXERCISE

Hold a round table discussion now with your study group on this whole question of our relationship with God. You may want to read the last few pages of *CWG*, Chapter 13, aloud, having one person read my words and others read the responses I received. Read from page 197 to the end of the chapter. That should take only about 15 minutes. In the discussion which follows, be sure to ask these questions:

- How does the information here square with your own belief system? How does it differ?
- What impact, if any, does this information have on your ideas about your relationship with God? What impact do you choose for it to have?
- If you could create a relationship with God in any way you wished, what would that look like for you?

If you are working alone with this Guidebook, answer the above questions in your journal after re-reading the pages noted.

Further discussion: *Have I not said "Ye are Gods?"*

Of course, the largest message of *CWG* is that all of us are Gods. Again, for many this is difficult to accept. Not so much because it does not seem likely that it could be true, but more often because of the responsibility it places upon all of us if it *is* true.

It is much easier for us to imagine ourselves as the *victim* of an unhappy life, not the *creator* of it; as being an *effect* of the world around us, not *at cause* in the matter.

We cannot imagine ourselves to be the *cause* of most of what we see going on around us. And perhaps individually we are not. Yet by extension – and through the ultimate logic of what evidences itself in the Truth that we are all One – we *are* creating what we are seeing. This point the text of *CWG* makes over and over again. And in *Book 2,* the point is made even more clearly as it regards planetary conditions, world events, and global consciousness. The time that it takes between cause and effect sometimes makes it difficult for us to see this relationship. We don't recognize (re-cognize: to *know again*) that we have, individually or through Collective Consciousness, caused that.

The truth is, as we look at the world around us, we cannot escape responsibility for any of it. Moreover, we would do better not to wish to. For as *CWG* says, only when we can accept responsibility for all of it can we begin to change any of it.

If "how things are" is no longer the experience we choose, then we must each work to change it. And we must begin today, for there is much to be done. It is as John Kennedy said over a quarter century ago. We may not be finished within the first 100 days, nor within the first 1,000 days, but let us begin.

If you have not read the second book in the *Conversations with God* trilogy, let me urge you right now to do so – right now.

CWG - Book 2 may be one of the most extraordinary documents to come along in a long time in the field of esoteric/spiritual/political/economic and social literature. In it, God invites us to create a revolution in our social, sexual, psychological, philosophical, educational, political, economical, and theological lives the likes of which has never before been visited upon this planet. A blueprint is presented for shifting the paradigm and changing the order of things; a blueprint which will turn everything topsy-turvey. . .but not upside down.

In fact, things will at last be *right side up.*

You're invited to take part in all this. Not as a bystander, but as a way-shower. Not as one of the changed, but as one of the changers.

It was John Kennedy's brother Bobby who uttered these word. . .words I hope I never forget:

> Some people see things as they are and ask, "Why?"
> I see things as they could be and ask, "Why not?"

to pause and reflect

ASSIGNMENT:

Start a Changer Journal right now. Decide to be one of The Changers, and place in the journal a notation each day. Design the pages to look like this:

What I did today to make my world better:

____

____

What I said today to make my world brighter:

____

____

What I shared today to make my world richer:

____

____

How I intend to use my life to change the world*:*

____

____

____

____

Additional Inquiries
from Chapter 13

1. What percentage of illness is self-created and what percentage is created by germs and/or accident?
2. What forms of mental activity cause most of our illnesses?
3. What attitude is required to heal the body once it is sick?
4. Name some ways to prevent illness.
5. How long could the body last if we cared for it properly?
6. Which is correct, Darwin's theory of evolution, or the Creationist theory?
7. What is the greatest barrier to our learning the truth?
8. The resurrection of Jesus is part of religious mythology which never really happened. *True or False?*
9. What is the ultimate secret regarding our true relationship to God?
10. There is nothing in reality, not even the "devil" or the dog poop on the grass, which is not part of God. *True or False?*
11. What is the only limit on what we can become?

Chapter 14
The Prayer That Never Ends

The fourteenth and final chapter of *CWG* is a rapid fire summary of the remaining of my questions asked earlier, but not covered before in the book. These questions are given brief answers. Some are covered in much greater detail in later installments of the trilogy, in particular the topic of sex in a major section of *Book 2*, and the subjects of karma, psychic ability, reincarnation, and life on other planets in *Book 3*.

This Guidebook's final chapter is likewise a summary, and likewise brief.

Perhaps the most impactful of the short commentaries comprising *CWG*'s closing chapter are the responses to my inquiries about human sexuality. In these replies I received a tiny glimpse of the mind-opening, heart-expanding, let-me-tell-you-what-it's-*really*-all-about explanations of human sexuality given to me in *Book 2*.

If the closing pages of *Book 1* lack great detail in the examination of sex, they lack nothing in candor. God tells us rather directly to play with sex, and that it was meant to be wonderful fun. It is something to *celebrate*, and to experience without shame. This, we are told pointedly, is not how most of the human family experiences it.

TEXT REFERENCE:

You have repressed sex, even as you have repressed life, rather than fully self expressing, with abandon and joy.

You have shamed sex, even as you have shamed life, calling it evil and wicked, rather than the highest gift and the greatest pleasure. — *Page 207*

What can we do about this now? How can we change things if we choose to? By knowing. . .

CONCEPT #34
All of life is a conversation with God.

God created nothing shameful. It is a shame that *we* have *created shame around the creations of God.*

We are so ashamed of our bodies that we will not let our children use the correct words for some of their most beautiful parts, and wouldn't dream of letting them see *our* parts.

We are so ashamed of that which attracts us to each other that we cover up (in most countries by law) every part of the body (in some countries, even the face) which could be defined as alluring, lest we fall prey to what we have for some reason chosen to call our basest desires.

We are so ashamed of our sexual functions that we perform them most often in the dark with a "Shhh! Don't let them *hear* you" attitude, rather than with sheer abandon and an openness which declares that this *is* a joyful celebration of life, and, yes, part of our ongoing conversation with God.

If the experience of your own sexuality has been even a little like this, it is possible you may wish to change that. The exercise below may help you to determine both your present attitudes about sex and whether or not you really wish to move into new sexual awareness, experience, and celebration.

EXERCISE

Answer the questionnaire below, being as open and honest as you can. You will not have to share your answers, but you will also not be restricted from doing so. The questions have to do with the more intimate and private aspects of your life. If you are uncomfortable answering the questions, do not do so.

Sexual Survey

1. When I was a child I was told about sex and how it works by my parents. *True* ___ *False* ___

2. I often saw my father or my mother nude, and seeing a naked body was not an unusual thing in our house, nor was it considered "inappropriate" or shameful. *True* ___ *False* ___

It is not considered inappropriate or shameful among family or loved ones in my present household either. *True* ___ *False* ___

3. The words vagina and penis were normal parts of my childhood vocabulary. *True* ___ *False* ___

4. My first sexual experience was (check as many as apply)

__ joyful __ scary __ damaging
__ something of which I felt ashamed
__ something about which I felt pleased and happy
__ experienced against my will
__ kept secret for a long time
__ openly and joyously acknowledged
__ just as I had always hoped and imagined it would be
__ a nightmare I am still not really over

5. Presently I find sex to be (check as many as apply)

__ a duty, more or less __ a pure joy
__ adventuresome __ actually, rather boring
__ less than what I'd really like __ just right as it is
__ something I seldom discuss with my children
__ something I openly discuss with my children
__ a little embarrassing to talk about with anybody
__ okay to talk about with almost anybody

6. I could watch an x-rated movie with explicit sexual activity and be totally comfortable. *True* ___ *False* ___

I would actually enjoy it. *True* ___ *False* ___

7. I am the mirrors-on-the-bedroom-ceiling type who celebrates my sexuality with earthy abandon. I love sex and don't mind saying it. *True* ___ *False* ___

8. I would go to an all nude beach any time.
True ___ *False* ___

9. I think nudist camps and sunbathing associations are unwholesome places and simply excuses for exhibitionists and voyeurs to take off their clothes. *True* ___ *False* ___

10. I think sex outside of marriage is natural and okay, enjoyed responsibly. *True* ___ *False* ___

11. If I could change the experience of my own sexuality that I am having today in any way, here's how I would have it be:

___

___

___

___

12. I think sex should be a private matter that is not best discussed this openly. Even completing this questionnaire was uncomfortable for me. *True* ___ *False* ___

Did you have any unusual response to this exercise? What did you feel as you were answering the questions? Did your answers tell you anything about yourself? Can you share this with your study group? If you are using this book individually, make an entry in your journal.

Further discussion: *The prayer that never ends*

I have taken to telling my audiences all across this country that life itself is a never-ending prayer. I believe that everything in life would change, and all the world would be better for it, if more people understood that.

Everything in life is a conversation with God – even the things we do in the dead of night, in the moments of our lustiest passion, as well as our most tender sharing.

If you can imagine God in your bedroom and still be comfortable, knowing that God is laughing, sharing, enjoying, caring, and experiencing *with* you the most vulnerable and intimate moments of your life, then you can imagine God in almost any other context as well – and that is good, because God is present in *every* context, and it about time we got used to having Her there.

No. It's larger than that. We would benefit from choosing it to be no other way.

So tomorrow, as you go through your day, think of your thoughts, your words, your every action as your end of a continuing Conversation with God. Through these devices and in this conversation, you declare who and what you are.

Are you pleased with the announcements you made yesterday? Are you hungry to make even grander announcements today? Are you inspired by your own ideas about tomorrow?

If not, why not?
If so, good for you.
And for us.

to pause and reflect

ASSIGNMENT:

This is your last assignment. In this final look at CWG through the eyes of this study guide, answer the questions below sometime during the next week. Come back next week prepared to discuss your answers. If there is to be no "next week" – if this is your last class – ponder your answers in the silence of your heart. And thank you for your willingness to study the CWG material more closely. You can only benefit from having done so.

Final Questionnaire

1. What do you think is the most important single message of CWG?
2. Did this book change you at all? If so, in what way?
3. What is, now, the grandest version of the greatest vision you have about yourself?
4. How often are you committed to having your own communication with God?

Additional Inquiries
from Chapter 14

1. We are not here to learn our spiritual lessons. *True or False?*
2. Life provides us a chance to pay off our karmic debt. *True or False?*
3. Psychic ability is real, and some people are "psychic" while others are not. *True or False?*
4. While sex is wonderful, lots of pictures of naked people having sex produces moral decay. *True or False?*
5. Is there life on other planets?
6. When will God leave us? What could cause Her to do so?

In Closing...

As I said in the dedication to this book, I am inspired by your willingness to take the time to delve more deeply into not just the truths, but the implications of the truths, in *CWG*, and how they could expand and transform your life. Although it is almost always exciting, the journey of self re-creation is rarely easy. Your decision to embark on this journey is a demonstration of courage and a commitment to growth which speaks volumes about who you are.

If this commitment leads you to seek even more information on these topics — particularly the *beingness vs. doingness* paradigm explored in Chapter 12 — I strongly recommend the booklets *Bringers of the Light* and *Recreating Yourself*. Focusing on only one area of the mass of material covered in this Guidebook, these smaller publications present a step-by-step approach to re-creating yourself anew in the grandest version of the greatest vision you ever had about Who You Are, and could be extremely useful as a supplement to this guide. Created as fund raisers to support our work, they are available for $11 each postpaid from our non-profit foundation, the address of which appears below.

Also available from the foundation is a monthly newsletter which contains an ongoing dialogue with readers of *CWG*. The exchanges in this regular forum include some of the most urgent and insightful questions I've been asked about the *CWG* material. The newsletter also contains updates on my workshop and lecture schedule, and — of particular interest to some readers of this Guidebook, I'm sure — a complete list of the current *CWG* Study groups by location and contact person. The monthly newsletter is $35 inside the U.S. And $45 outside the U.S. (In U.S. Dollars only) for 12 consecutive issues, with scholarship subscriptions availaable upon request. You may contact our foundation at:

ReCreation, PMB # 1150, 1257 Siskiyou Blvd., Ashland, Oregon 97502
Toll-free order line: (877) 740-0230
email: recreating @aol.com
website: www.conversationswithgod.org

I do not want to end our visit together here without giving you a little report on the document which so many of you have called "your book," and my recommendation on some others I hope you will read.

I have been deeply moved by the response to *Conversations with God*. We are now receiving hundreds of letters each week from people all over the world who tell us their lives have been touched in very special and indelible ways by the *CWG* dialogues. As I write this, those dialogues are being translated into 20 languages and the U.S. edition has been high on *The New York Times* bestseller list for five months.

Something remarkable is going on here. I believe it is something which can change the world. First, by changing the world's idea about God, then by changing the world's idea about itself. What I notice is that God has always asked us to balance faith and works.

In the *CWG* trilogy we are invited to bring into existence a world in which more and more people have the opportunity to experience God's presence and to understand the virtually unlimited opportunities of life on this planet. Robert Theobald has been writing about the challenges of the twenty-first century for the last forty years. He has just summarized his understandings and proposals in a short, easy-to-read book, *Reworking Success: New Communities at the Millennium* (New Society Publishers). You may not find this little volume readily available in your bookstore, but you can order it. I hope that you will. It provides a scenario for what Robert believes must happen in the years around the turn of the century if we are to move in positive directions. I personally invite your attention to this man and his insights. I have found both to be extraordinary.

Also a must-read is the latest book from wonderful Marianne Williamson, *The Healing of America* (Simon & Schuster). Please do not miss it. Marianne is one of the angels' messengers, sent to wake us up.

As I have often said before, in my own books and to audiences everywhere, I believe that our most wonderful days on this planet are still ahead of us. If this assessment turns out to be accurate, it will be because of you, and thousands of others like you, who have found such value in the *CWG* material that you have chosen to share it with others, and to render it functional in your life.

We walk a convergent path, and it is good to have your company.

With love and great hope
for our tomorrows,

NEALE DONALD WALSCH
Ashland, Oregon

Answers to Study Guide Review Questions

Following each answer is the page number in *Conversation with God – Book 1* on which the subject will be found, together with more information on the subject.

CHAPTER 1

1. Thoughts, feelings, experience, and words. (3)
2. God's answer is always the highest thought, the clearest word, the grandest feeling. (4)
3. Some people listen and others don't. (7-8)
4. Because asking for something is a statement that you do not now have it. Since your Word is Law, this statement becomes your reality. (11)
5. Because thought is prayer, and it is often your Sponsoring Thought which is being "answered." When your Sponsoring Thought opposes your in-the-moment wish, it will appear as if God is not answering your prayer. (12)
6. False. God does not create. You do. (13)
7. That God cares what we do; that the outcome of life is in doubt. (13-14)
8. Love and Fear. (15, 18-19)
9. It is the thought behind the thought behind the thought. (16)
10. To turn its grandest concept about itself into its greatest experience. (22)
11. So that we could have something to compare ourselves to, and thus know and experience Who We Really Are. (22-26)
12. You cannot know yourself as Tall unless and until you become aware of Short. You cannot experience Fat unless you've experienced Thin. In the realm of the Relative, a thing cannot exist except in the space of its opposite. Everything exists relative to something else. (27-28, 31)
13. God the Father is *knowing*, God the Son, *experiencing*, God the Holy Spirit, *being*. (30)
14. Knowing, experiencing, being. (30)

15. Gross: everything has an opposite; Sublime: nothing has an opposite. (31)
16. So that It could experience Itself as the Light. (33-34)
17. As a statement to the universe of Who You Are. (36)
18. Neither. They are the result of mass consciousness. (37)
19. Whatever we want to do about them. Yet judge not, and neither condemn. (38)
20. Unfulfillment; knowing Who and What You Are and failing to experience that. (40)
21. No. (41-42)
22. Because that would break the law: allow each soul to walk its path. (46-47)
23. Fear is an emotion; emotion is energy-in-motion; like energy attracts like energy. (54)
24. Thought is creative; fear attracts like energy; love is all there is. (56)

CHAPTER 2

1. God has no gender, is neither male nor female. (59-60)
2. Nothing. (60-61)
3. Nothing. (61)
4. That which you call evil. (61)
5. To allow yourself to become what you are because of the experience of others. (62)
6. God does not want them at all. (64)
7. Desire. (65)
8. Joyful, loving, accepting, blessing, grateful. (65-66)
9. Hold onto them so long as they serve you. Yet look to see if they create the best idea about you. (66)
10. False. (67)

CHAPTER 3

1. To ask for what we want, and to understand the process of the asking and the answering. (73)
2. Thought, word and action. (74)
3. To make it possible for us to fully experience who we really are (the Creator) by creating ourselves anew. This would not be possible without forgetfulness. (75)
4. He gets the experience through us. (75) (also, 99)
5. First, you must choose for your life to "take off" by believing

and living the promise of God that you are God's equal. Second, accept that your world is the result of your idea about it. Third, think, speak and act as the God that you are. (75-76)

6. Your life will offer more beauty, more comfort, more peace, more joy, and more love of self and others. (76)
7. Imagine your life the way you want it to be. Make sure every thought, word and action is in harmony with that desire. Move away from any thought, word, or action which is not. (77-78)
8. . . .stop making value judgments. Stop calling a thing "good" or "bad." Then, notice that all conditions are temporary. Nothing stays the same, nothing remains static. Which way a thing changes depends on you. (79)
9. The soul's desire is to experience the highest feeling of love. (83)
10. False. For the soul to experience perfect love it must experience every human feeling. (83)
11. It lengthens the journey to reawakening. (86)
12. False. You are good and you are Godly, and acceptance of that is the shortest path.

CHAPTER 4

1. There is no way we can do this. Our return to God is guaranteed. (88)
2. Because life is not a process of discovery, it is a process of creation. (90-91)
3. Thought, word, and deed. (91)
4. The place of knowing is the place of gratitude. (91)
5. Because to condemn it is to condemn yourself, since you created it. (92)
6. Because we are operating unconsciously – that is, unaware that our thoughts are creating our reality. (92)
7. Think about what you think about. Constantly monitor your thoughts. Throw out those you don't want. (92-93)

CHAPTER 5

1. There is no one true path to God. All paths lead to the same destination. (94)
2. They are God's promises (the Ten Commitments) as to how we can know we have found the path to God. They are God's announcements of how we will act when we become One with God once again. (96-97)

3. Heaven is everywhere, which means heaven is nowhere in particular. . .which means heaven is now/here. (98)
4. We can't experience what we don't know. . .and we don't know what we haven't experienced. (99)
5. False. But not following them may be. (101)
6. Expectation. (102)
7. Because when you resist something you make its illusion real. And what you resist persists. (102)
8. To create who and what you are, and then experience that. (104)

CHAPTER 6

1. He has. We are not using the tools. (106)
2. You cannot know and become that which you are in the absence of that which you are not. (107)
3. Our judgments. (108)
4. Live them and see if they work. (109)

CHAPTER 7

1. It is the process of conscious creation – creation with a purpose – undertaken moment to moment. (113)
2. Provide them with the means to become independent. (114)
3. False. True Masters have the fewest students, for they have turned them all into Masters. Only false masters keep students subjugated in studenthood. (114)
4. c. (117)
5. God has no role in creating our lives. God simply empowers us to conjure whatever we choose. (118)
6. c. (118)
7. Read and re-read *CWG* until its truths replace the false teachings in our mind. (120)

CHAPTER 8

1. To provide you with the opportunity to create, know, and experience who you really are. (122)
2. Most people in couples are concerned with what the other is thinking, doing, having instead of what they are "being" in relationship to it. (124)
3. False. (125)
4. False. (124-125)

5. c. (124-125)
6. Admit honestly how you are feeling. Tell the truth. Don't "hide out." (128)
7. True. (128)
8. Body. (130)
9. Soul. (130)
10. Love. (130)
11. a. (130)
12. Determining what you are trying to do in that moment, and determining your purpose in life. (132)
13. It could be, if you wish to stop a despot. (132-133)
14. Of course. Without that which you define as evil, that which you call good cannot exist. (134)
15. There are none. (135)
16. False. (136)
17. False. (138)
18. See page 141.

CHAPTER 9

1. True. (149)
2. No. Yet, if you agree with the highest moral law human beings have devised, you will always do so. (151)
3. Your own authority. (153)
4. You cannot answer this question incorrectly.
5. False. (155)
6. There is nothing else to do! (155)
7. Life has no built-in purpose. The purpose of life is the purpose you give it. (157)
8. No. In fact, it is a sign of your evolution. (157)

CHAPTER 10

1. Chapter 10 is the answer to everything.

CHAPTER 11

1. A belief that money is "bad"; undervaluing things we call "good"; the belief in lack, or "not enoughness." (162)
2. Do the deed you want to have the new thought about; say the words you want to have the new thought about. (164)
3. From the experience of others. (165)

4. False. Her joy comes from our freedom, not our compliance. (166)

CHAPTER 12

1. "Doing" is a function of the body; "being" is a function of the soul. (170)
2. True. (170)
3. False. (174)
4. The soul provides us with the opportunity to experience what we want, and the mind chooses either that experience or another (174), the body acts out the choice. (175)
5. False. Obedience can never produce salvation. (175)
6. When body, mind and soul operate in harmony (175)
7. False. The very act of wanting something creates the lack of it. (178)
8. Gratitude (180)
9. False. We do not drop the body. It changes form, and we take all but the densest part. (181)
10. The soul. (182)
11. False. God *never* judges us. (183)
12. Nothing. (187)
13. False. (186)

CHAPTER 13

1. All illness is self-created. (187)
2. Worry, hate and fear. (188)
3. Faith, or "absolute knowing" (189)
4. Change our thinking from fear to love; take better care of our bodies through exercise, diet, and abstinence from toxic substances such as drugs and alcohol. (190)
5. Forever. (193)
6. Both. (195)
7. Our idea that we already know it. (196)
8. False. It happened. (196)
9. We are the body of God. (197)
10. True. (200)
11. It does not exist. There is no limit. (201)

CHAPTER 14

1. True. (203)
2. False. We have no such debt. (204)

3. False. There is no one who is not psychic. (205)
4. True. Or False. Whatever you say. Pictures of naked people having sex are simply pictures of naked people having sex. You decide what they mean to you, whether they are "okay" or "not okay."
5. Of course. (208)
6. Never. Nothing. (211)

For a limited edition reprint of the original cover painting by Louis Jones, please write to:

Hampton Roads Publishing Company
publishes and distributes books on a variety of subjects,
including metaphysics, health, complementary medicine,
visionary fiction, and other related topics.

To order or receive a copy of our latest catalog, call toll-free,
(800) 766-8009, or send your name and address to:

Hampton Roads Publishing Company, Inc.
134 Burgess Lane
Charlottesville, VA 22902